A
Berkshire
Christmas

Compiled by David Green

ALAN SUTTON PUBLISHING LIMITED

BERKSHIRE BOOKS

First published in 1994
Alan Sutton Publishing Limited · Phoenix Mill · Far Thrupp
Stroud · Gloucestershire
in association with
Berkshire Books

British Library Cataloguing in Publication Data

A catalogue record for this book is available from the
British Library.

ISBN 0-7509-0596-4

BERKSHIRE BOOKS
Publishing imprint of Berkshire County Council
Managed by Alan Sutton Publishing Limited

Cover illustration: On the way to Dingley Dell, *by Francis James
Barraud (courtesy of N.R. Omell Gallery; photograph: Fine Art
Photographic Library Ltd)*

Typeset in Garamond 12/13.
Typesetting and origination by
Alan Sutton Publishing Limited.
Printed in Great Britain by
Ebenezer Baylis, Worcester.

Contents

Preface

In compiling this anthology, I have inevitably had to acknowledge the fact that the Berkshire we know today is a somewhat different county from that which existed before 1974. In the boundary changes of that year, Berkshire lost to Oxfordshire its northernmost towns and villages in the Vale of the White Horse, but gained from Buckinghamshire a new swath of territory to the east, including towns like Slough and Eton. In effect, this has given me two Berkshires – the old and the new – from which to select material for inclusion, and both are represented in these pages.

DAVID GREEN

from

Beyond the Village Green

MABEL COPPINS

*The story of one woman's life in the Berkshire village of
Holyport, near Maidenhead, was written by Mabel
Coppins in the early 1980s. It is a fascinating account of
the day-to-day happenings in a close-knit rural
community, spanning the period from the years of
depression after the First World War, to the very changed
character of village life in modern times. Her vivid
recollections of the simple Christmas celebrations of her
childhood have a special appeal, as the following extract
illustrates.*

Christmas was quite a happy time, even though we didn't
have the expensive gifts the children have today. If we were
very lucky we had an apple, an orange, a bar of chocolate and
a bag of sweets, and if some kind person gave us a tin of
toffees, well, that was beyond our wildest dreams.

But we did have the luxury of a chicken for our
Christmas dinner, a turkey being far beyond the means of
most cottage homes. Occasionally some kind employer
gave one as a Christmas present, but very few did, I can
tell you.

Then we would have some tinned fruit, or maybe some nuts, for these things appeared in the shops only at Christmas, and not every family could afford them.

One year my father won a goose in a raffle, and we had a wonderful Christmas, but I do remember my mother saying, 'Oh, what a lot of grease!' This found its way, I feel sure, on to slices of bread to feed us children long into the New Year.

Outings at Christmas were very rare indeed, at least in our family. We never had the pleasure of going to see a pantomime, and parties among the poorer families of the village were few and far between, since nearly everyone found it hard to make ends meet anyway, without the added problem of feeding other people's children.

My father being a building worker, through no fault of his own often found himself out of work during the festive season, with only the meagre dole money to struggle by on.

However, we did have one particular treat to look forward to – a visit to our Aunt Isobel, who lived in a wonderful thatched cottage at Fifield. This was a ritual every Boxing Day without fail. We'd set out from home to walk there in the partial darkness of the late afternoon, to arrive in good time for tea. And we knew exactly what we'd get: seedy cake, Madeira cake, plain bread and butter, and bread and home-made jam. A very dull and uninteresting tea was had by all!

Aunt Isobel was a small Victorian figure, with white hair and a long black dress which reached the ground. It was pulled in very tightly at the waist. She wore white lace round her neck, and a big spotlessly white apron. She was very abrupt, to say the least, with little or no sense of humour.

After tea, and with a glass of home-made elderberry wine clasped in our tiny hands, we waited for our annual treat, the playing of the musical box. As we sat watching, as quiet as little mice, Aunt Isobel unwrapped the precious machine from its black velvet bag. Soon the cottage was alive with

tinkling music as Aunt put on record after record, from 'The Grand Old Duke of York' to 'Lily of Laguna'.

But it always ended much too soon, and despite our protests – 'Please, one more, Aunt Isobel' – the musical box was whisked away until Boxing Day the following year. Then, as if by some form of consolation, she would give us another small portion of wine, followed by medlars.

I'm sure many of you have tasted the delight of a medlar, but for those of you who haven't, perhaps I can describe it. It's actually like a small pear, or perhaps I should say a rotten pear, for that's exactly what it looks like. They grew on a tree in Aunt Isobel's orchard and were rare even in those days, so I'm pretty sure they must be almost extinct by now.

Then Father would look at his watch and say it was time to go home, with something special to talk about when we got back to school. Already we were looking forward to Boxing Day the following year, when once again we could listen to Aunt Isobel's musical box.

It was at this time of year that we'd go sliding on the frozen ponds. Our favourite place was The Lake, which was in one of the fields in front of our house. First we would make sure the ice would bear our weight, then we set about sliding from one end to the other, seeing who could cut the biggest marks on the ice. This we called 'making candles'.

You could only do this if you had studs on your boots, and most children wore boots in my day so that they might stand up to the vast amount of walking we had to do. Mind you, if Father caught us we were in trouble, for boots, although very cheap by modern standards, were still beyond the pockets of most cottage families and required saving up for.

In fact, most people bought them on the 'never-never' from the 'Tally Man' who called regularly. My word! Haven't things changed, for in those days, to get something on tick was very much frowned upon and branded you as the poorest

of the poor. Now, of course, it's very much an accepted part of living, and I suppose it's true to say that most people are living on credit, one way or another.

When it was dark, and when we'd had our tea and wrapped ourselves up well against the cold, we'd set off once again for the lake. But this time we were armed with empty jam jars and a pocketful of household candles. These, by the way, were the standard form of lighting in most of the cottages, together with oil lamps, so they were easy to get hold of and quite cheap, and our parents didn't mind us taking one or two. In fact, it was a recognised thing, that everyone in the gang brought their own candles for the night's activity – ice hockey.

First, we would set the lighted candles in the jam jars and place them round the edge of our lake, and then toss for sides. Then, with sticks taken from a hedge nearby, and an old tin for a puck, play would begin.

Soon, shrieks of laughter would echo through the crisp cold air as we slithered over the ice of our floodlit arena, eyes aglow with excitement as we tried to slide the puck between the opposing team's goal posts, usually two coats laid on the ice.

Then, all too soon, Mother's familiar voice would come floating across the field, calling us home for supper and bed. For a while we would tarry, and then one by one the candles in the jars were blown out and we'd make our way home through the darkness to the hole in the hedge opposite the cottage, tired and glowing with youthful good health from our efforts.

Mother always managed to have something hot for us to drink, and then we would creep up the stairs to bed, with a flickering candle to show us the way.

from
Old English Customs

P.H.DITCHFIELD

When the prolific Berkshire writer Peter Hampson Ditchfield wrote Old English Customs *in 1896, he was the Rector of Barkham near Wokingham. His object was to describe all the old customs 'which still linger on in the obscure nooks and corners of our native land', recording only those 'which time has spared', and mourning the large number which had died out. He noted that some of the old traditions of Christmas had survived better than most, and he devoted considerable space in his book to explaining them. Since then, several more have passed into obscurity as a result of changing social attitudes over the past century – as these extracts from Ditchfield's Christmas chapters reveal.*

All the old poets sing in praise of the great festival of the Saviour's birth, which, according to Herrick, 'sees December turned to May', and makes 'the chilling winter's morn smile like a field beset with corn'.

Sir Walter Scott bewails the decline of the ancient modes of celebrating the festival, and says:

'The yule log is no longer drawn in state into the baron's hall . . .'

> England was merry England when
> Old Christmas brought his sports again;
> A Christmas gambol oft would cheer
> A poor man's heart through all the year.

The 'Lord of Misrule' has been dead many years and been decently buried, though when alive he did not always merit that epithet. The yule log is no longer drawn in state into the baron's hall, but we have still some fragments of ancient revels preserved in the mummers' curious performance.

Carol singing is very general in most parts of England, but few of the old carols are sung. 'Good King Wenceslas' and other modern carols or hymns have supplanted the ancient

traditional ones. The singing of carols is a memorial of the hymn sung by the angels to the shepherds at Bethlehem. In some places the children carry round a doll laid in a box, a rude representation of the Holy Child in his manger bed.

The mistletoe is still hung in our houses at Christmastime, but few connect this instrument of mirth with the wild beliefs of our Norse ancestors. The mistletoe plays an important part in Scandinavian mythology, and the custom of hanging branches of this plant is common to all Norse nations.

The legend is that Baldur was slain by a mistletoe dart at the instigation of Loki; and in reparation for this injury the plant is dedicated to his mother Frigg, so long as it does not touch the earth, which is Loki's kingdom. Hence the mistletoe is hung from ceilings in our houses, and the kiss given under it is a sign that it is no longer an instrument of mischief.

Some contend that kissing under the mistletoe is a dead or dying custom; others state that all kissing should be abandoned on the grounds that it spreads infection. It is perhaps difficult to arrive at any safe conclusion with regard to the prevalence of this particular custom, as those who practise it are not always the most forward in proclaiming their adherence to primitive usages.

Among the foods peculiar to special seasons, none is so common as the plum pudding at Christmas. 'Time immemorial' is the usual period assigned for the introduction of practices about which knowledge is limited, and the date of the invention of Christmas plum puddings has been relegated to that somewhat vague and indefinite period.

But the plum pudding is not older than the early years of the eighteenth century, and appears to be a 'House of Hanover' or 'Act of Settlement' dish. The pre-Revolution or Stuart preparation of plums and other ingredients was a

porridge or pottage, and not a pudding, and was made with very strong broth of shin of beef.

The searchers of the symbolical interpretations contend that on account of the richness of its ingredients, the plum pudding is emblematical of the offerings of the Wise Men. The same authorities assert that mince pies, on account of their shape, are symbolical of the manger bed of the Infant Saviour. I venture to think that such interpretations should be received with some hesitation.

The children still delight in their Christmas tree, which also belongs to no 'immemorial time', the first Christmas tree being introduced to this country by some German merchants who lived in Manchester. The Queen and Prince Albert have

Since Victorian times, Christmas trees have brought 'endless delights to each succeeding generation of children'

also celebrated Christmas with its beautiful old German custom; and the Court having set the fashion, Christmas trees became general, and have brought endless delights to each succeeding generation of children.

The festivals associated with the Christmas period have some old customs. On St Thomas's Day (21 December) the custom of mumping is still practised in many places, where the old women perambulate the town and are accustomed to receiving small gratuities. The word *mumping* comes to us from the Dutch, and signifies to *mumble* or *mutter*. The beggars on this occasion are usually old people, and toothless age mumbles both food and words; hence the beggars are called *mumpers*, and they are said to go a-mumping.

In many parts of the country it is called 'going a-gooding' or 'going a-Thomasing', and in some places the money collected is given to the vicar and churchwardens, who distribute it to the poor aged folk on the Sunday after St Thomas's day.

Before the days of the Society for the Prevention of Cruelty to Animals, boys were accustomed, in many places, to kill wrens and carry them about on furze bushes from house to house, repeating the words:

> The wren, the wren, the king of the birds,
> St Stephen's Day was killed in the furze;
> Although he be little his family's great,
> And so good people, give us a treat.

The origin of the cruel custom is curious. There is a Norse legend of a beautiful siren who bewitched men and lured them into the sea. A charm was obtained to counteract her evil influence and capture the siren, who contrived to escape by assuming the form of a wren. Once every year, presumably on St Stephen's Day, she was compelled by a powerful spell to

appear in the guise of the bird, and ultimately to be slaughtered by mortal hand.

Hence poor wrens have been killed in the hope of effecting the destruction of the beautiful siren. The feathers of the birds were plucked and preserved as a prevention from death by shipwreck, and formerly its body was placed in a bier, and buried with much solemnity in a grave in the churchyard, while dirges were sung over its last resting-place.

Fanciful interpreters have seen in the stoning of the wren a connection with the stoning of St Stephen, whose martyrdom occurred on the day of the observance of this barbarous custom.

Another legend is that one of St Stephen's guards was awakened by a bird just as his prisoner was about to escape.

The wren, once killed as part of a traditional Christmas ritual

Children still look forward to the Christmas pantomime, which, in spite of modern developments, maintains its popularity, especially in the provinces.

Pantomimes have entirely changed their character since they were first introduced into this country in 1702. The humours of Grimaldi and his successors, the merry tricks of the clown and the diversions of the harlequinade, have given place to grand spectacular displays and scenic effects which would certainly have astonished our forefathers. However, the pantomime will probably long continue to hold its place on the list of Christmas customs.

The day after Christmas is still known as Boxing Day, and is so called from the Christmas boxes which used to be in circulation. In the British Museum are specimens of 'thrift boxes' – small and wide bottles with imitation stoppers, from three to four inches in height, of thin clay, the upper part

The first English Christmas card was issued in 1846

covered with a green glaze. On one side is a slit for the introduction of money, and as the small presents were collected at Christmas in these money pots, they were called Christmas boxes.

Thus these boxes gave the name to the present itself and to the day when these gifts were commonly made.

The sending of Christmas cards is a very popular custom, which shows no sign of decay. The custom is of very recent growth, the first English Christmas card being issued in 1846. The design was drawn by J.C. Horsley, R.A, at the suggestion of Sir Henry Cole, KCB, representing a merry family party gathered round a table quaffing generous draughts of wine.

The sale of a thousand copies of this card was then considered a large circulation. Since those days the custom has become universal. If good wishes could bring us happiness, our cups of joy would indeed be full, and 'a Merry Christmas and a Happy New Year' would fall to the lot of all, except to the postmen.

It is tempting to wonder what Peter Ditchfield would make of our present-day Christmas customs, a century after he wrote his book. Overriding commercialism and the homage we pay to the television set would almost certainly jar his religious sensibilities, and he would no doubt find incredulous our all-pervading multi-million Christmas card ritual which has developed from the tentative beginnings he described. At least he might find some comfort in the fact that the postman is no longer obliged to work on Christmas Day.

Holly and Ivy

TRADITIONAL

Many of England's traditional folk songs have been preserved for posterity through the efforts of such assiduous collectors as Ralph Vaughan Williams and Cecil Sharp. No less enthusiastic in his study of the subject was Alfred Williams, who concentrated his research mainly on the upper Thames Valley from Reading westward to the river's source. Within this area, he made a close study of the wealth of old regional ballads and songs which had been handed down from generation to generation, many of them, by the early years of the present century, in danger of being lost. In 1923 a selection of these was published in Folk Songs of the Upper Thames, *from which the following – the first of three examples reproduced in these pages – is taken. It is a song for the festive season, and Williams records that he heard it in many of the Thames Valley villages.*

My father left me a good acre of land –
   Sing holly, sing ivy;
My father left me a good acre of land,
And a bunch of green holly and ivy.

I ploughed it up with a team of rats –
   Sing holly, sing ivy;
I ploughed it up with a team of rats,
And a bunch of green holly and ivy.

Gathering in the holly and the ivy

I harrowed it with a small-toothed comb –
   Sing holly, sing ivy;
I harrowed it with a small-toothed comb,
And a bunch of green holly and ivy.

I sowed some peppercorns and they came up –
   Sing holly, sing ivy;
I sowed some peppercorns and they came up,
And a bunch of green holly and ivy.

I reaped it with my little penknife –
   Sing holly, sing ivy;
I reaped it with my little penknife,
And a bunch of green holly and ivy.

I thrashed it with a little beanstalk –
    Sing holly, sing ivy;
I thrashed it with a little beanstalk,
And a bunch of green holly and ivy.

I winnowed it with the tail of my shirt –
    Sing holly, sing ivy;
I winnowed it with the tail of my shirt,
And a bunch of green holly and ivy.

I sent it to market with a team of rats –
    Sing holly, sing ivy;
I sent it to market with a team of rats,
And a bunch of green holly and ivy.

The rats they all came galloping back –
    Sing holly, sing ivy;
The rats they all came galloping back,
And a bunch of green holly and ivy.

from

The Wind in the Willows

KENNETH GRAHAME

Kenneth Grahame lived from 1859 to 1933 and for much of his life Berkshire was his home. As a child he lived at Cookham Dean by the Thames, as well as Cranbourne, returning to the former in adulthood. At other times he had homes at Blewbury on the Berkshire Downs and in the Thames-side village of Pangbourne, and it was from his knowledge and love of the river that he drew so much inspiration when he came to write The Wind in the Willows. *The story evolved from the spontaneous bedtime tales about the creatures of the river bank which he related to his son Alastair, and it has since become one of the best-loved classics of children's literature. The book provides this first extract from Kenneth Grahame's writings. The scene is Mole End, the cosy subterranean home that Mole was beginning to fear he would never find again on this dark and snowy night a few days before Christmas. But after much sobbing and self-reproach, and with the help of the indefatigable Rat, the little dwelling was eventually rediscovered.*

The Rat was running here and there, opening doors, inspecting rooms and cupboards, and lighting lamps and candles and sticking them up everywhere.

'What a capital little house this is!' he called out cheerily. 'So compact! So well planned! Everything here and everything in its place! We'll make a jolly night of it. The first thing we want is a good fire; I'll see to that — I always know where to find things. So this is the parlour? Splendid! Your own idea, those little sleeping bunks in the wall? Capital! Now, I'll fetch the wood and the coals, and you get a duster, Mole — you'll find one in the drawer of the kitchen table — and try and smarten things up a bit. Bustle about, old chap!'

Encouraged by his inspiriting companion, the Mole roused himself and dusted and polished with energy and heartiness, while the Rat, running to and fro with armfuls of fuel, soon had a cheerful blaze roaring up the chimney. He hailed the Mole to come and warm himself; but Mole promptly had another fit of the blues, dropping down on a couch in dark despair and burying his face in his duster.

'Rat,' he moaned, 'how about your supper, you poor, cold, hungry, weary animal? I've nothing to give you — nothing — not a crumb!'

'What a fellow you are for giving in!' said the Rat reproachfully. 'Why, only just now I saw a sardine-opener on the kitchen dresser, quite distinctly; and everybody knows that means there are sardines about somewhere in the neighbourhood. Rouse yourself! Pull yourself together, and come with me and forage.'

They went and foraged accordingly, hunting through every cupboard and turning out every drawer. The result was not so very depressing after all, though of course it might have been better; a tin of sardines — a box of captain's biscuits, nearly full — and a German sausage encased in silver paper.

'There's a banquet for you!' observed the Rat, as he arranged the table. 'I know some animals who would give their ears to be sitting down to supper with us tonight!'

'No bread!' groaned the Mole dolorously; 'no butter, no . . .'

'No *pâté de foie gras*, no champagne!' continued the Rat, grinning. 'And that reminds me – what's that little door at the end of the passage? Your cellar, of course! Every luxury in this house! Just you wait a minute.'

He made for the cellar door, and presently reappeared, somewhat dusty, with a bottle of beer in each paw and another under each arm. 'Self-indulgent begger you seem to be, Mole,' he observed. 'Deny yourself nothing. This is really the jolliest little place I ever was in. Now, wherever did you pick up these prints? Make the place look so home-like, they do. No wonder you're so fond of it, Mole. Tell us all about it, and how you came to make it what it is.'

Then, while the Rat busied himself fetching plates and knives and forks, and mustard which he mixed in an egg cup, the Mole, his bosom still heaving with the stress of his recent emotion, related – somewhat shyly at first, but with more freedom as he warmed to his subject – how this was planned, and how that was thought out, and how this was got through a windfall from an aunt, and that was a wonderful find and a bargain, and this other thing was bought out of laborious savings and a certain amount of 'going without'.

His spirits finally quite restored, he must needs go and caress his possessions, and take a lamp and show off their points to his visitor and expatiate on them, quite forgetful of the supper they both so much needed; Rat, who was desperately hungry but strove to conceal it, nodding seriously, examining with a puckered brow, and saying, 'Wonderful', and 'Most remarkable', at intervals, when the chance for an observation was given him.

At last the Rat succeeded in decoying him to the table, and had just got seriously to work with the sardine-opener, when sounds were heard from the forecourt without – sounds like

the scuffling of small feet in the gravel and a confused murmur of tiny voices, while broken sentences reached them – 'Now, all in a line – hold the lantern up a bit, Tommy – clear your throats first – no coughing after I say one, two, three. Where's young Bill? Here, come on, do, we're all a'waiting.'

'What's up?' inquired the Rat, pausing in his labours.

'I think it must be the fieldmice,' replied the Mole, with a touch of pride in his manner. 'They go round carol-singing regularly at this time of the year. They're quite an institution in these parts. And they never pass me over – they come to Mole End last of all; and I used to give them hot drinks, and supper too sometimes, when I could afford it. It will be like old times to hear them again.'

'Let's have a look at them!' cried the Rat, jumping up and running to the door.

It was a pretty sight, and a seasonable one, that met their eyes when they flung the door open. In the forecourt, lit by the dim rays of a horn lantern, some eight or ten little fieldmice stood in a semicircle, red worsted comforters round their throats, their fore-paws thrust deep into their pockets, their feet jigging for warmth.

With bright beady eyes they glanced shyly at each other, sniggering a little, sniffing and applying coat-sleeves a good deal. As the door opened, one of the elder ones that carried the lantern was just saying, 'Now then, one, two, three!' and forthwith their shrill little voices uprose on the air, singing one of the old-time carols that their forefathers composed in fields that were fallow and held by frost, or when snowbound in chimney corners, and handed down to be sung in the miry street to lamp-lit windows at Yuletime.

A contemporary portrait of
Kenneth Grahame
by John S. Sargent, RA

CAROL

Villagers all, this frosty tide,
Let your doors swing open wide,
Though wind may follow, and snow beside,
Yet draw us in by your fire to bide;
Joy shall be yours in the morning.

Here we stand in the cold and the sleet,
Blowing fingers and stamping feet,
Come from far away you to greet –
You by the fire and we in the street –
Bidding you joy in the morning.

For ere one half of the night was gone,
Sudden a star has led us on,
Raining bliss and benison –
Bliss tomorrow and more anon,
Joy for every morning!

Goodman Joseph toiled through the snow –
Saw a star o'er a stable low;
Mary she might not further go –
Welcome thatch, and litter below!
Joy was hers in the morning!

And then they heard the angels tell
'Who were the first to cry Nowell?
Animals all, as it befell,
In the stable where they did dwell!
Joy shall be theirs in the morning!'

The voices ceased, the singers, bashful but smiling, exchanged sidelong glances, and silence succeeded – but for a moment only. Then, from up above and far away, down the tunnel they had so lately travelled, was borne to their ears in a faint musical hum the sound of distant bells ringing a joyful and clangorous peel.

'Very well sung, boys!' cried the Rat heartily. 'And now come along in, all of you, and warm yourselves by the fire, and have something hot!'

'Yes, come along fieldmice,' cried the Mole eagerly. 'This is quite like old times! Shut the door after you. Pull up that settle to the fire. Now just you wait a minute while we – O Ratty!' he cried in despair, plumping down on a seat, with tears impending. 'Whatever are we doing? We've nothing to give them!'

'You leave all that to me,' said the masterful Rat. 'Here, you with the lantern! Come over this way. I want to talk to

you. Now, tell me, are there any shops open at this hour of the night?'

'Why, certainly, sir,' replied the fieldmouse respectfully. 'At this time of the year our shops keep open to all sorts of hours.'

'Then look here!' said the Rat. 'You go off at once, you and your lantern, and you get me . . .'

Here much muttered conversation ensued, and the Mole only heard bits of it, such as – 'Fresh, mind! – No, a pound of that will do – see you get Buggins's, for I won't have any other – no, only the best – if you can't get it there, try somewhere else – yes, of course, home-made, no tinned stuff – well then, do the best you can!' Finally, there was a clink of coins passing from paw to paw, the fieldmouse was provided with an ample basket for his purchases, and off he hurried, he and his lantern.

The rest of the fieldmice, perched in a row on the settle, their small legs swinging, gave themselves up to enjoyment of the fire, and toasted their chilblains till they tingled; while the Mole, failing to draw them into easy conversation, plunged into family history and made each of them recite the names of his numerous brothers, who were too young, it appeared, to be allowed to go out a'carolling this year, but looked forward very shortly to winning the parental consent.

The Rat, meanwhile, was busy examining the label on one of the beer bottles. 'I perceive this to be Old Burton,' he remarked approvingly. 'Sensible Mole! The very thing! Now we shall be able to mull some ale! Get the things ready, Mole, while I draw the corks.'

It did not take long to prepare the brew and thrust the tin heater well into the red heart of the fire; and soon every fieldmouse was sipping and coughing and choking (for a little mulled ale goes a long way) and wiping his eyes and laughing and forgetting he had ever been cold in all his life.

'They act plays too, these fellows,' the Mole explained to the Rat. 'Make them up all by themselves, and act them afterwards. And very well they do it, too! They gave us a capital one last year, about a fieldmouse who was captured at sea by a Barbary corsair, and made to row in a galley; and when he escaped and got home again, his lady-love had gone into a convent. Here you! You were in it, I remember. Get up and recite a bit.'

The fieldmouse addressed got up on his legs, giggled shyly, looked round the room, and remained absolutely tongue-tied. His comrades cheered him on, Mole coaxed and encouraged him, and the Rat went so far as to take him by the shoulders and shake him; but nothing could overcome his stagefright.

They were all busily engaged on him like water men applying the Royal Humane Society's regulations to a case of long submersion, when the latch clicked, the door opened, and the fieldmouse with the lantern reappeared, staggering under the weight of his basket.

There was no more talk of play-acting once the very real and solid contents of the basket had been tumbled out on the table. Under the generalship of Rat, everybody was set to do something or to fetch something. In a very few minutes supper was ready, and Mole, as he took the head of the table in a sort of dream, saw a lately barren board set thick with savoury comforts; saw his little friends' faces brighten and beam as they fell to without delay; and then let himself loose – for he was famished indeed – on the provender so magically provided, thinking what a happy homecoming this had turned out, after all.

As they ate, they talked of old times, and the fieldmice gave him the local gossip, up to date, and answered as well as they could the hundred questions he had to ask them. The Rat said little or nothing, only taking care that each guest

had what he wanted, and plenty of it, and that Mole had no trouble or anxiety about anything.

They clattered off at last, very grateful and showering wishes of the season, with their jacket pockets stuffed with remembrances for the small brothers and sisters at home. When the door had closed on the last of them and the chink of the lantern had died away, Mole and Rat kicked the fire up, drew their chairs in, brewed themselves a last nightcap of mulled ale, and discussed the events of the long day.

At last the Rat, with a tremendous yawn, said, 'Mole, old chap, I'm ready to drop. Sleepy is simply not the word. That your own bunk over on that side? Very well, then, I'll take this. What a ripping little house this is! Everything so handy!'

He clambered into his bunk and rolled himself well up in the blankets, and slumber gathered him forthwith, as a swath of barley is folded into the arms of the reaping machine.

The weary Mole also was glad to turn in without delay, and soon had his head on his pillow, in great joy and contentment.

from

Memories of Old Berkshire

JANE M. TAYLOR

Jane Taylor spent the whole of her life on a Berkshire farm, and she was in her seventy-ninth year when she so evocatively penned her recollections in Memories of Old Berkshire. *One of a family of ten children, she was able to cast her mind back as far as the severe winter of 1881 when the snowdrifts were hedge-high, and she could vividly recall the celebrations for Queen Victoria's Jubilee in 1887. In the following extract from her book she describes the simple pleasures of the typical farmhouse Christmases of her childhood, long before rampant commercialism and the television set changed the character of the festive season for ever.*

Christmas in those far-away days was very often a white one — not always snowy, but what was lovelier still, with a sparkling hoar frost.

About ten days before Christmas the excitement began. Every evening as we sat round the fire, with shutters bolted and curtains drawn, we children would wonder, 'Who will come tonight?' Then up the gravel path outside the windows we would hear the slow tramp of heavy feet, and after a few

minutes' delay for whispered instructions, up would strike the village brass band.

Instead of the usual 'Rule Britannia' or 'Two Little Girls in Blue', they would play the good old Christmas hymns like 'While Shepherds Watched' and 'Hark! The Herald Angels Sing'. After a good long programme they would pause, hoping the door would open and money be handed out — which, of course, always happened.

Another evening the handbell ringers would come. I think I hear them now, the sweet tones of the bells ringing out on the frosty air.

Various small bands of children also sang hymns and simple carols, hoping for money for Christmas fare. They were not disappointed, as the spirit of generosity was abroad. But the real carol singers were men and women from the church and chapel choirs. They practised for weeks, and although untrained, sang most beautifully, not in unison but all taking their separate parts.

They would stand in a circle, with the light from their horn lanterns shining on their solemn rapt faces. The light was dim, being only from home-made tallow candles, but they were used to dark nights and unlighted roads, and knew all the words by heart.

Carol singing was their offering to the celebration of Christ's birthday. But to us children the highspot of Christmas entertainment was the visit of the mummers. About eight or nine men would arrive outside the house, and strike up with:

> God bless the master of this house,
> We hope he is within.
> And if he is, pray tell us so
> And us'll soon step in.
> We hopes the mistress is within,

> A-settin' by the fire,
> An' pitying us poor mummers, yer
> Out in the mud and mire.
> We don't come 'ere but once a year
> And hope 'tis no offence,
> But if it is, pray tell us so
> And we will soon go hence.
> For we be come this Christmas time
> Our purpose to be merry.

My father would then open the door and invite them into our large paved kitchen, and the show would begin, watched with bated breath by all of us ten children, our parents, the maids, and any visitors there might be.

The mummers were led by Father Christmas in the correct attire and with a long white beard. He stumped around, leaning on his stick and reciting:

> Christmas comes but once a year
> And when it comes, it brings good cheer,
> Roast beef, plum pudden, mince pies.
> The geese are getting fat,
> Please to put a penny in the old man's hat.

Then he would introduce 'King George' – a fine, upstanding young man (incidentally, the village gamekeeper) resplendent in a navy blue uniform and much yellow braid. He was asked to fight the 'Turk', who proved to be a man with a very black face and a very odd costume.

They immediately set to, and after much sword play and dodging round and round the ring, the 'Turk' fell to the ground, lying silent and still. Father Christmas then called, 'Is there a doctor to be found?' and out stepped a man in a long black coat and top hat. From his black bag he took a

'Christmas in those far-away days was very often a white one . . .' –
an early photograph of Beenham Church in a picturesque setting of
snow and hoar frost

bottle, and said, 'In this bottle I have medicine to cure the
itch, the stitch, the palsy and the gout; pains within, and
pains without. I drop a drop into the palm of the dead man's
hand, and a drop on his tongue, and say to him, "Turk, arise,
and get thee back to thine own country"!'

The cure was instantaneous. The 'Turk' arose and joined the
rest of the company, who all added something to the play. I
remember one little fat man who always had a row of dolls of
various sizes on his back. He would say:

> In come I, little happy Jack,
> With my wife and my family on my back.
> My head he's big, but my wits are small,
> So I brought my fiddle to please 'ee all.

28

Then they all danced round until large jugs of beer appeared, and a huge dish of mince pies — made specially for the occasion.

The theme of the play, no doubt, dated back to the Middle Ages, and it varied from county to county. In our village the play carried on very successfully until the First World War.

Those were happy days! Everybody in the village contributed something to the spirit of Christmas, if only by collecting holly and ivy for decorating the church, where on Christmas morning the men, women and children met to praise the new-born King and to wish each other the old, old wish, 'A Merry Christmas'.

from

Village Christmas

MISS READ

'Miss Read' is the nom de plume *of the writer Dora Saint whose home is in the Berkshire countryside near Newbury. Her many delightful books on life in the country continue to earn her wide popularity, and her stories evoke vivid memories of the days when rural life proceeded at a gentler pace than today, and there was more time to savour the simple pleasures which brightened the workaday lives of country folk. In* Village Christmas, *Miss Read takes us into her charming fictional*

*village of Fairacre, as it prepares for the festive season. In this
extract we meet the two kindly spinster sisters Mary and
Margaret Waters, who live in Flint Cottage. Christmas Day is
almost here . . .*

The next three days were busy ones for the ladies at Flint
Cottage. Red-berried holly, pale mistletoe and glossy ivy were
collected, and used to decorate the living room. Two red
candles stood one at each end of the mantlepiece, and a holly
garland hung from the brass knocker on the front door.

The cake was iced, the pudding fetched down from the top
shelf in the pantry, the mincemeat jar stood ready for the pies
and a trifle was made. One of Mrs Pringle's chickens arrived
ready for the table, and sausage meat came from the butcher.

Margaret crept away privately while Mary was bringing in
logs from the woodshed, and wrapped up two pairs of sensible
lisle stockings which she had bought at Caxley for her sister's
present. Mary took advantage of Margaret's absence at the Post
Office and swiftly wrapped up a pair of stout leather gloves
and hid them in the second drawer of the bedroom chest.

All Fairacre was abustle. Margaret and Mary helped to set up
the Christmas crib in the chancel of St Patrick's church. The
figures of Joseph, Mary and the Child, the shepherds and the wise
men reappeared every year, standing in the straw provided by Mr
Roberts the farmer, and lit with sombre beauty by discreetly
placed electric lights. The children came in on their way from
school to see this perennial scene, and never tired of looking.

The sisters helped to decorate the church too. There were
Christmas roses on the altar, their pearly beauty set off by
sprigs of dark yew amidst the gleaming silver ware.

On Christmas Eve the carol singers set out on their annual
pilgrimage round the village. Mr Annett, the choirmaster,
was in charge of the church choir and any other willing
chorister who volunteered to join the party. This year, the

'Margaret and Mary opened
their window and watched the
singers at work . . .'

newcomer Mr Emery was among them, for word had soon
gone round that he sang well and Mr Annett had invited him
to join the carol singers. Clad in the duffle coat which Mr
Willet thought of so poorly, he strode cheerfully along the
frosty lanes of Fairacre, swinging the hurricane lamp as
though he had lived in the village all his life . . .

One of their stopping places was outside The Beetle and
Wedge, strategically placed in the village street. Margaret and
Mary opened their window and watched the singers at work.
Their breath rose in silver clouds in the light of the lanterns.
The white music sheets fluttered in the icy wind which spoke of
future snow to the weather-wise of Fairacre. Some of the lamps
were hung on tall stout ash sticks, and these swayed above the
ruffled hair of the men and the hooded heads of the women.

Mr Annett conducted vigorously and the singing was

controlled as well as robust. As the country voices carolled the eternal story of joyous birth, Mary felt that she had never been so happy. Across the road she could see the upstairs light in the bedroom of the Emery children, and against the glowing pane were silhouetted two dark heads.

How excited they must be, thought Mary! The stockings would be hanging limply over the bed rail, just as her own and Margaret's used to hang so many years ago. There was nothing to touch the exquisite anticipation of Christmas Eve.

> 'Hark the herald angels sing,
> Glory to the new-born King',

fluted the choirboys, their eyes on Mr Annett, their mouths like dark Os in the lamplight. And the sound of their singing rose like incense to the thousands of stars above.

from

Windsor Forest

ALEXANDER POPE

One of the greatest of English poets and essayists, Alexander Pope lived from 1688 to 1744. Although he was largely self-educated and suffered a severe childhood illness which stunted

*his growth, he produced many epic literary works including his
celebrated* Essay on Criticism, Essay on Man *and* The
Rape of the Lock. *For much of his life he lived with his
parents at Binfield in the Windsor Forest, a setting which
provided inspiration for the subject-matter – and title – of
another of his major works.* Windsor Forest *was first
published in 1713, and the following extract is an expressive
winter cameo which typifies the eloquence and mastery of
language that have earned Pope his undisputed place in
English literary history.*

See! from the brake the whirring pheasant springs,
And mounts exulting on triumphant wings:
Short is his joy; he feels the fiery wound,
Flutters in blood, and panting beats the ground.

'When hoary winter cloaths
the year in white . . .' – a
Berkshire lane in all its
seasonal beauty

Ah! what avail his glossy, varying dyes,
His purple crest, and scarlet-circled eyes,
The vivid green his shining plumes unfold,
His painted wings, and breast that flames with gold?
When hoary winter cloaths the year in white,
The woods and fields to pleasing toils invite.
To plains with well-breath'd beagles we repair,
And trace the mazes of the circling hare:
(Beasts, urg'd by us, their fellow-beasts pursue,
And learn of man each other to undo.)
With slaught'ring guns th' unwearied fowler roves,
When frosts have whiten'd all the naked groves;
Where doves in flocks the leafless trees o'ershade,
And lonely woodcocks haunt the wat'ry glade.
He lifts the tube, and levels with his eye;
Straight a short thunder breaks the frozen sky:
Oft, as in airy rings they skim the heath,
The clam'rous lapwings feel the leaden death:
Oft, as the mounting larks their notes prepare,
They fall, and leave their little lives in air.

The Christmas Mummers

JOHN NORTON

The colourful rural custom of performing Christmas mummers' plays is an ancient one and, as writer John Norton describes here, it was once common throughout Britain. But, although its popularity has declined, it has survived in a few locations up and down the country, including Berkshire.

Like many of our Christmas customs, mumming – the word is derived from the German *mumme* or mask – almost certainly owes its origin to the bizarre practices of the pagan Roman festival of Saturnalia, in which masquerading in curious costumes was an inseparable part of the proceedings.

The early Christians, although sharply disapproving of what they saw as undesirable heathen behaviour, decided that the best way to counter it was to adopt a policy of 'if you can't beat them, join them'. So they donned masks and allowed themselves to indulge in just a little of the less offensive frolicking, not as a gesture of acquiescence, but in an attempt to pour ridicule on what was going on.

The church authorities soon saw a chance to turn the whole ritual to their own advantage, and gradually introduced elements of a more spiritual nature into the annual junketing. Eventually, what had begun as purely pagan occasions,

developed into the early Christian 'mystery' or 'miracle' plays, and it was as offshoots of these that the Christmas mumming plays became popular.

Ironically, over the centuries, the religious characters which had become an intrinsic element of the plays, gradually gave way to characters from popular legend and even pagan mythology, and these, in one form or another, have survived right up to modern times. But one essentially Christian element of the plot which has never changed, is the triumph of good over evil, of life over death.

Although the mumming plays which have survived into the present century in various parts of the country are all very

An early drawing of Victorian mummers. On the left is Father Christmas, his face masked and his hat bedecked with holly. In his hands he holds a wassail bowl

similar, they do differ in detail depending upon the interpretation of the groups of mummers performing them. They all have a basic core of four principal characters – Father Christmas, King George, the Turkish Knight and the Noble Doctor. But individual groups of performers have often introduced additional characters, either to embellish the story or to add a touch of local colour.

King George is thought to be a corruption of Saint George of dragon-slaying fame, while the Turkish Knight may be an echo from the Crusades. Father Christmas is, of course, an obligatory character considering the time of year when the plays are performed, and the Noble Doctor is the personification of good over evil.

Berkshire's mummers seem to have been among those who liked to bring in various additional personalities peculiar to the county. In the 1930s, for instance, the mummers who were regularly performing in Whitley on the outskirts of Reading, introduced three colourful characters called Bold Roamer, Twing-Twang and Johnny Jack, who all played their part in enacting the basic story.

In the 1960s, a Reading resident who had been a mummer sixty years earlier, recalled some of his experiences in a letter to a local newspaper. 'We always started our performances two weeks before Christmas,' he wrote, 'and, weather permitting, would go round the public houses every night until Christmas Eve.'

No mention was made of the name of his particular mummers' group, but whoever they were, they too introduced their own additions to the *dramatis personae* in the form of Bold Slasher, Joe the Sweep and Old Mother Sack.

In the modern and more sophisticated world in which we now live, when the television set is our primary form of entertainment even over Christmas, it is difficult to appreciate the importance which village communities once attached to the visits of the mummers to the local inns during the festive

season. The plays, although as familiar to most people as their own names, were eagerly awaited, and the performances were a colourful annual highspot in the lives of hard-working rural communities. After all, before the advent of public transport and the private motorcar, village folk rarely had the opportunity to seek entertainment outside their own locality, and the mummers were therefore guaranteed large and appreciative audiences.

At one time there were groups of mummers in every corner of Berkshire, some of them visiting several neighbouring villages apart from their own. It was, of course, in their interest to perform in as many locations as possible, whether these were inns or private houses, as they were sure to find most people imbued with the Christmas spirit, and therefore not ungenerous with their donations. An added bonus was that at each inn where they performed, more than a few tankards of ale were consumed as necessary refreshment. As a result, their performances no doubt became increasingly rumbustious as the evening progressed.

Unfortunately, records of many of the old Berkshire mummers are now no longer in existence, although a few village histories and other documents do survive to confirm the wide appeal which this fascinating old custom once enjoyed.

In the 1880s, for instance, there were regular performances of mummers' plays in the village of Compton between Reading and Wantage, and at Steventon near Abingdon. The Berkshire Downs village of Brightwalton had its mummers too, and so did Burghclere, just over the Hampshire border near Newbury.

A fascinating old document among the parish records for Walton near Newbury mentions a mummers' play in the hamlet of Hoe Benham, which was performed each Christmas until at least 1900. It is given its full rather grand title of 'The Christmas Mummers Play of King George', and includes the four basic characters of King George, Father Christmas, the

Turkish Knight (also known here as Foreign King), and the Noble Doctor who in this play is given the name Peter Gray.

In the custom of the time, the Hoe Benham Mummers also introduced a few characters of their own, to add a touch of variety to the story-telling. There's a colourful fellow called Tall and Smart, and a curious character by the name of Bold Granny Dear which is thought to be a corruption of 'Bold Grenadier'.

Then there's the sprightly Happy Jack whose sole job appears to be encouraging the audience to ply the troupe with money and ale, spurred on by the play's final character, an itinerant fiddler rejoicing in the name of Mazzant Binnit. This is evidently another corruption, this time based on the fact that this particular player is the last one to appear and is therefore 'Him as aint been yet'.

Such delightful corruptions are not really surprising, as the mummers often consisted of country folk with little or no education who were largely illiterate. With their rich rural dialect, an inability to write other than phonetically, and performances which were usually well lubricated with strong ale, it is easy to see how, over a period of time, 'Bold Grenadier' became 'Bold Granny Dear', and 'Him as aint been yet' was reduced to 'Mazzant Binnit'.

Here, then, is the text of the traditional mummers' play as performed at Hoe Benham around the turn of the century, based on the original hand-written version which presumably, and thankfully, was recorded by someone who had the benefit of some sort of formal education –

Enter Father Christmas, saying –

> In comes I, old Father Christmas,
> Welcome or not,
> And I hope old Father Christmas
> Will never be forgot.

Christmas comes but once a year
And when it comes it brings good cheer.
Roast beef, plum pudding, mince pies –
Who likes them better, Happy Jack or I?
In this room there shall be shown
The greatest battle that ever was known:
Between King George and the Turkish Knight
Come in to Old England for to fight.
A room, a room, I do pursue,
With my brave boys and soldier too;
And that is the reason why I say
Walk in King George and clear the way.

Enter King George.

In come I King George,
That man of courage bold.
With my broad sword in my hand
I won ten thousand pounds in gold.
'Twas I that fought the fiery dragon
And brought him to the slaughter,
'Twas I that won the King of Egypt's daughter,
With menials so brave and varlets so true.
I have cowered armies and nations,
How bold it is to say
I will fight any fighting man that comes within my way.

Enter the Foreign King.

In comes the Foreign King,
With my broad sword in my hand I will quickly make
     it swing –
Likewise I am the bold Turkish Knight,
Just returned to Old England for to fight.

Let King George, that man of courage bold,
Draw his sword: if his blood does heat
I will quickly make it cool.

K.G.   Hold thou Turkish Knight!
Thou talkest very bold.
But draw thou sword and fight,
Or draw thy purse and pay,
For satisfaction I will have
Afore thou goes away.

T.K.   Satisfaction! King George, there is no satisfaction at all, for thee and I will battle to see which of us on the floor shall first fall.

They fight. T.K. is beaten to his knee.

T.K.   Pardon me, pardon me this once I pray!
Pardon me King George and for ever I will be thy slave!

They fight. T.K. is killed.

F.C.   Oh king, oh king, what hast thou done?
Thou has ruined me by killing my only son!

K.G.   Nay, father, 'twas thy son as gave me the first challenge.

F.C.   Is there a doctor to be found,
To cure this man lying bleeding and wounded on the ground?

K.G.   Yes, there is a doctor to be found,
To cure this man lying wounded and bleeding on the ground.

F.C.   Who is he?

K.G.   Peter Gray.

Enter Peter Gray.

P.G.   Who are you a-calling Peter Gray?
       My name is Mister Gray,
       So the people all say.

F.C.   Oh doctor, doctor, what is thy fee?

P.G.   Ten guineas is my fee,
       But fifty will I take of thee.

F.C.   Take it all, doctor, but what canst thou cure?

P.G.   I can cure the itch and the stitch, the pousy and the gout,
       All pains within and all pains without,
       And if this man's got a bush in his toe,
       I can pull him out.
       Yes, I am a little noble doctor; I am not one of the
       deceitful doctors as walk about from one place to the
       other. What I do I does before you all, ladies and
       gentlemen; 'tis hard if you can't believe your own eyes.
       I've got a bottle here called the foster drops. I'll put one
       drop on the tip of his tongue and one drop on the palm
       of his hand, and I will say to him 'Arise, arise, and walk
       gently as thou canst.'

K.G.   Arise, arise, and get thee back to thine own country,
       and tell them that King George can fight ten thousand
       better men than thee.

The Blewbury Mummers enact their Christmas play, a colourful
perpetuation of an ancient custom

F.C.   Walk in Tall and Smart.

Enter Tall and Smart.

T.S.   In comes I, both Tall and Smart,
         I tell my mind with all my heart.
         My head is made of iron,
         My body's lined with steel,
         My trousers fits my legs so tight,
         My garters drags my heels.
         First comes Christmas and then comes Spring,
         I am a little jolly lad that can either dance or sing.

F.C.   Walk in Bold Granny Dear.

Enter Bold Granny Dear.

B.G.   In comes I Bold Granny Dear,
For Tall and Smart I do not fear.
If his head is made of iron
And his body lined with steel,
From his head to his shoulders
I will quickly make him feel.

F.C.   Walk in Happy Jack.

Enter Happy Jack.

H.J.   In come I little Happy Jack,
With my wife and family at my back.
My family large though I am small,
Little helps us all.
Out of nine I got but five,
And half of they are starved alive.
A cup of Christmas ale will make us dance and sing,
But money in our pockets is a much better thing.
Ladies and gentlemen, sitting at your ease,
Give us a little Christmas box, just what you please.

F.C.   Walk in Mazzant Binnit.

Enter Mazzant Binnit.

M.B.   In comes I as aint been yet,
With my big head and little wit.
My head so big, my wit so small,
I comes with my fiddle to please you all.
Blue sleeves, yellow lace,

All you mummers dance a pace.
The fiddler in a great distress
For want of a little money.

And so the play ended, with the audience being persuaded to dip into pockets and purses, and the landlord urged to top up the ale tankards before the mummers moved on to their next call.

Such performances were once an inseparable part of English rural life at Christmastime, and it is a tribute to the traditionalists and students of folklore in our modern times that the plays have not been allowed to die out entirely.

In the village of Blewbury, for instance, one group of mummers still survives, and is faithfully perpetuating a custom which is unquestionably a unique part of our rural heritage. As Christmas arrives, so they don their traditional costumes and make-up, and take their play to the four village inns, and sometimes to a neighbouring village as well. Their performances are injected with all the enthusiasm and gusto which have characterised mummers' plays for countless generations. Long may this splendid old tradition flourish.

Yule Times

QUEENIE RIDEOUT

In 1986 the Wargrave Local History Society published The Book of Wargrave, *a wide-ranging collection of historical notes*

A Berkshire Christmas

and reminiscences contributed by people living in and around this attractive Thames-side village. Among the contributors was Queenie Rideout, whose memories of Christmases in the 1930s and 1940s, reproduced here in slightly abridged form, provide one of the book's most fascinating chapters.

Christmas in Wargrave now is not so very different from the 1930s, apart from the fact that there are many more people and fewer shops.

We were well catered for in the High Street in those days, having two large grocery shops, a butcher, greengrocer, dairy, ladies' and gents' hairdressers, W.H. Smith & Sons, a Post Office, a bakery in Church Street, a confectioner and chemist. The Post Office sold a good range of ladies' and gents' wear including shoes and underwear.

Almost all the shops were well stocked with Christmas gifts at reasonable prices. Half-hourly buses ran to Henley (6d return fare) and Reading (11d return fare). A journey to Reading to see Father Christmas was a 'must' for the children, who delighted in doing their own private shopping at that time.

Mums and dads went to Woolworth's for pillow case fillers – those wonderful toy sweet shops, bus conductors' sets, nurses' outfits and toy Post Offices which could all be purchased for less than 10 shillings the lot. One more expensive present was usually bought for each child, costing about a pound.

At home, weeks before the day, all the family gathered round the kitchen table preparing the ingredients for the Christmas puddings and mincemeat. A large bowl of water was necessary for little sticky fingers busy stoning raisins, and then came the big stir with a large wooden spoon, and the threepenny pieces were dropped into the mixture.

Evenings were spent making paper chains for decorations. Carol singers were out in force, vying with each other for customers. Houses were not crowded together as they are now,

A Reading poulterer well-stocked with Christmas fare in 1951

so it was necessary to sing one verse of a carol quickly, then ring the bell and away to the next house. Sometimes there was a hold-up, as the occupier requested 'another verse to be sung more slowly please'.

Party giving seemed to go on for weeks, but the big event was the school Christmas party and the Christmas tree hung with a present for each child, and books for good work through the year.

Then came the war years with rationing, blackout and gas masks. Not to be outdone, families coped, and rations were pooled to give the children treats. Christmas puddings had grated carrots and apples and dried eggs added instead of rich fruits. A very small issue of dried fruit for each household

helped. Mashed parsnip with a few drops of banana essence made a good substitute for real bananas.

A lovely Christmas party was given in the Woodclyffe Hall by the firemen of the village, who worked tirelessly all through the war years. Whilst waiting for calls, they made toys for the children out of tin cans, pieces of wood, bottle tops and cotton reels. Somehow, they collected enough rations for a tea party, ending with toys from a Christmas tree, tea and entertainment. It was a great effort by all concerned.

The Christmas pantomimes went on as usual, the children rehearsing their dance routines and learning their lines. Some unrehearsed incidents happened of course – such as one plump Flower Fairy getting stuck in her flowerpot; one Fairy Sun who would not smile, and one who got carried away with delight and just had to show all the frills Mum had sewn on her pants, so one pretty bottom was shown to the audience!

However, *The Sleeping Beauty, Dick Whittington, Aladdin* and *Jack and the Beanstalk* all went ahead successfully. I remember Dick's cow crying all over the audience when she was to be sold; Aladdin's grotto full of jewels; and Jack's mum climbing the beanstalk to rescue him!

Will today's children have similar memories of the Wargrave Theatre Workshop productions?

Another contributor to The Book of Wargrave *was Edie Fry whose reminiscences are centred on the nearby hamlet curiously known as Crazies Hill. This unusual name, the book informs us, has numerous possible derivations, one of which attributes its origin to the local abundance of poppies and buttercups, both of which were once known as 'crazies'. In the case of buttercups, the name is supposed to have alluded to the fact that their scent could induce madness in anyone who smelled them. Other more prosaic explanations are that the word 'crazies' is from the French* crassier *meaning 'slag heap' or, more likely, from the French for 'chalk',* craie. *Crazies Hill is indeed a*

hill of chalk. But whatever the origin of its name, the hamlet is still as attractive today as it was in the years following the First World War when, as Edie Fry recalls, carol singing was one of the memorable highlights of the Christmas season for the local children.

Christmas time in Crazies Hill was really something. As most of the village kids went carol singing, we would meet up and see what each other had made. But I thought of a plan where we could excel the others. We took Mum's tablespoons out of the drawer, tied string round them and hung them on a stick. Then I tapped them with a wooden spoon to make them sound like bells.

The first big house we went to belonged to a Captain. As soon as we started up he opened the door and let four dogs out who chased us up the drive. I dropped the spoons and we had to wait behind the fence until they called the dogs in, so that we could get Mum's spoons back.

'A journey to Reading was a must . . .' – a wintry scene in the town
on Christmas Day in 1927

But the night we went to Sir Campbell Rhodes' big house, Hennerton, the door opened and a beautiful young girl of about twelve said, 'Will you come into the drawing room and sing to my uncle?'

Imagine four little girls with red noses and muddy shoes, Dad's old army socks full of holes on our hands for gloves, and our little mate Arthur Goodwin holding the glass lantern with a smoking candle, standing on an almost white carpet.

Sir Campbell was lying on a lovely brocaded settee, his hands folded across his chest as if he were dead. He listened with eyes closed as we sang carol after carol, and then he got up, went out, and returned with a big orange and half a crown each.

We made nine shillings and twopence each that night, and gave it all to Mum to buy Christmas goodies.

from

Our Village

MARY RUSSELL MITFORD

Mary Russell Mitford was a country writer of rare insight, with an ability to reflect with remarkable sincerity the rural way of life she knew so well in the early 1800s. She was born a few days before Christmas in 1787, and for much of her life she lived at Three Mile Cross not far from Reading. She died at Swallowfield in 1855. One of her most emotive books is **Our**

A Berkshire Christmas

Village, *based not on one specific place, but drawing on her intimate experience of several Berkshire communities. In this first extract, she describes, with an often poetic eloquence, a country walk during a bitter spell of winter weather.*

At noon today I and my white greyhound Mayflower set out for a walk into a very beautiful world — a sort of silent fairyland — a creation of that matchless magician the hoar frost. There had been just snow enough to cover the earth and all its colours with one sheet of pure and uniform white, and just time enough since the snow had fallen to allow the hedges to be freed of their fleecy load, and clothed with a delicate coating of rime.

The atmosphere was deliciously calm; soft, even mild, in spite of the thermometer; no perceptible air, but a stillness that might almost be felt; the sky, rather grey than blue, throwing out in bold relief the snow-covered roofs of our village, and the rimy trees that rise above them, and the sun shining dimly as through a veil, giving a pale fair light, like the moon, only brighter.

There was a silence, too, that might become the moon, as we stood at our little gate looking up the quiet street; a sabbath-like pause of work and play, rare on a workday; nothing was audible but the pleasant hum of frost, that low monotonous sound, which is perhaps the nearest approach that life and nature can make to absolute silence.

The very wagons, as they come down the hill along the beaten track of crisp yellowish frost-dust, glide along like shadows; even May's bounding footsteps, at her height of glee and speed, fall like snow upon snow.

But we shall hear noise enough presently: May has stopped at Lizzy's door! and Lizzy, as she sat on the window-sill with her bright rosy face laughing through the casement, has seen her and disappeared. She is coming. No! The key is turning in

the door, and sounds of evil omen issue through the keyhole —
sturdy 'Let me outs' and 'I will goes', mixed with shrill cries
on May and on me from Lizzy, piercing through a low
continuous harangue, of which the prominent parts are
apologies, chilblains, sliding, broken bones, lollipops, rods,
and gingerbread, from Lizzy's careful mother.

'Don't scratch the door, May! Don't roar so, my Lizzy!
We'll call for you as we come back.'

'I'll go now! Let me out! I will go!' are the last words of
Miss Lizzy.

I do think her mother might have let the poor little soul
walk with us today. Nothing worse for children than
coddling. Nothing better for chilblains than exercise. Besides,
I don't believe she has any — and as to breaking her bones in
sliding, I don't suppose there's a slide on the common.

These murmuring cogitations have brought us up the hill,
and halfway across the light and airy common, with its bright
expanse of snow and its clusters of cottages, whose turf fires
send such wreaths of smoke sailing up the air, and diffuse
such aromatic fragrance around.

And now comes the delightful sound of childish voices,
ringing with glee and merriment almost from beneath our
feet. Ah, Lizzy, your mother was right! They are shouting
from that deep irregular pool, all glass now, where, on two
long, smooth, liny slides, half a dozen ragged urchins are
slipping along in tottering triumph.

Half a dozen steps bring us to the bank right above them.
May can hardly resist the temptation of joining her friends,
for most of the varlets are of her acquaintance, especially the
rogue who leads the slide — he with the brimless hat, whose
bronzed complexion and white flaxen hair, reversing the usual
lights and shadows of the human countenance, give so strange
and foreign a look to his flat and comic features.

This hobgoblin, Jack Rapley by name, is May's great crony;

and she stands on the brink of the steep irregular descent, her black eyes fixed full upon him, as if she intended him the favour of jumping on his head.

She does: she is down, and upon him, but Jack Rapley is not easily to be knocked off his feet. He saw her coming, and in the moment of her leap sprang dexterously off the slide on the rough ice, steadying himself by the shoulder of the next in the file, which unlucky follower, thus unexpectedly checked in his career, fell plump backwards, knocking down the rest of the line like a nest of card-houses.

There is no harm done; but there they lie, roaring, kicking, sprawling, in every attitude of comic distress, whilst Jack

'A very beautiful world' – snow and hoar frost paint a wintry picture at Sindlesham, an area of Berkshire which Mary Russell Mitford loved and knew well

Rapley and Mayflower, sole authors of this calamity, stand apart from the throng, fondling, and coquetting, and complimenting each other, and very visibly laughing, May in her black eyes, Jack in his wide close-shut mouth and his whole monkey-face, at their comrades' mischances.

I think, Miss May, you may as well come up again, and leave Master Rapley to fight your battles. He'll get out of the scrape. He is a rustic wit, a sort of Robin Goodfellow, the sauciest, idlest, cleverest, best-natured boy in the parish; always foremost in mischief, and always ready to do a good turn.

The sages of our village predict sad things of Jack Rapley, so that I am sometimes a little ashamed to confess, before wise people, that I have a lurking predilection for him (in common with other naughty ones), and that I like to hear him talk to May, almost as well as she does.

'Come, May!' and up she springs, as light as a bird. The road is gay now: carts and post-chaises, and girls in red cloaks, and, afar off, looking almost like a toy, the coach. It meets us fast and soon. How much happier the walkers look than the riders — especially the frost-bitten gentleman, and the shivering lady with the invisible face, sole passengers of that commodious machine! Hooded, veiled and bonneted as she is, one sees from her attitude how miserable she would look uncovered.

Another pond and another noise of children. More sliding? Oh, no! This is a sport of higher pretension. Our good neighbour, the lieutenant, skating, and his own pretty little boys, and two or three other four-year-old elves, standing on the brink in an ecstasy of joy and wonder.

Oh, what happy spectators! And what a happy performer! They admiring, he admired, with an ardour and sincerity never excited by all the quadrilles and the spread-eagles of the Seine and the Serpentine. He really skates well though, and I am glad I came this way; for, with all the father's feelings

sitting gaily at his heart, it must still gratify the pride of skill to have one spectator at that solitary pond who has seen skating before.

Now we have reached the trees – the beautiful trees! – never so beautiful as today. Imagine the effect of a straight and regular double avenue of oaks, nearly a mile long, arching overhead, and closing into perspective like the roof and columns of a cathedral, every tree and branch encrusted with the bright and delicate congelation of hoar frost, white and pure as snow, delicate and defined as carved ivory.

How beautiful it is, how uniform, how various, how filling, how satiating to the eye and to the mind – above all, how melancholy! There is a thrilling awfulness, an intense feeling of simple power in that naked and colourless beauty, which falls on the earth like the thoughts of death – death pure, and glorious, and smiling – but still death. Sculpture has always the same effect on my imagination, and painting never. Colour is life.

We are now at the end of this magnificent avenue, and at the top of a steep eminence commanding a wide view over four counties – a landscape of snow. A deep lane leads abruptly down the hill; a mere narrow cart-track, sinking between high banks clothed with fern, and furze, and low broom, crowned with luxuriant hedgerows, and famous for their summer smell of thyme.

How lovely these banks are now – the tall weeds and the gorse fixed and stiffened in the hoar frost, which fringes round the bright prickly holly, the pendent foliage of the bramble, and the deep orange leaves of the pollard oaks! Oh, this is rime in its loveliest form! And there is still a berry here and there on the holly, 'blushing in its natural coral' through the delicate tracery, still a stray hip or haw for the birds, who abound here always.

The poor birds, how tame they are, how sadly tame! There is the beautiful and rare crested wren, perched in the middle

of the hedge, nestling as it were amongst the cold bare boughs, seeking, poor pretty thing, for the warmth it will not find. And there, farther on just under the bank, by the slender runlet, which still trickles between its transparent fantastic margin of thin ice, as if it were a thing of life — there, with a swift, scudding motion, flits, in short low flights, the gorgeous kingfisher, its magnificent plumage of scarlet and blue flashing in the sun, like the glories of some tropical bird.

He is come for water to this little spring by the hillside — water which even his long bill and slender head can hardly reach, so nearly do the fantastic forms of those garland-like icy margins meet over the tiny stream beneath. It is rarely that one sees the shy beauty so close or so long: and it is pleasant to see him in the grace and beauty of his natural liberty, the only way to look at a bird.

We used, before we lived in a street, to fix a little board outside the parlour window, and cover it with breadcrumbs in the hard weather. It was quite delightful to see the pretty things come and feed, to conquer their shyness, and do away with their mistrust. First came the more social tribes, 'the robin redbreasts and the wren', cautiously, suspiciously, picking up a crumb on the wing, with the little keen bright eye fixed on the window; then they would stop for two pecks; then stay till they were satisfied.

The shyer birds, tamed by their example, came next; and at last one saucy fellow of a blackbird — a sad glutton, he would clear the board in two minutes — used to tap his yellow bill against the window for more. How we loved the fearless confidence of that fine frank-hearted creature! And surely he loved us. I wonder the practice is not more general.

'May! May! naughty May!' She has frightened away the kingfisher; and now, in her coaxing penitence, she is covering me with snow. 'Come, pretty May! It is time to go home.'

A Royal Christmas at Windsor

FROM QUEEN VICTORIA'S PERSONAL JOURNALS

When, in 1841, Prince Albert first introduced Christmas trees to the seasonal celebrations at Windsor Castle, he started a custom which rapidly spread throughout the nation and has characterized the festive season ever since. Christmas trees certainly played an important part in the royal family's celebrations of 1850, as Queen Victoria noted in the daily entries in her Journals. These entries, which provide a fascinating insight into life at Windsor Castle during the Christmas period almost 150 years ago, are reproduced here exactly as they were written, with numerous examples of the Queen's own shorthand and abbreviations which she would have found useful in compiling so comprehensive and detailed a document.

24th December 1850. Windsor Castle.

The frost gone, & a raw dull morning. Albert out shooting, & I, walking with the Children. We walked out in the afternoon, & found it raw & damp. We began, by giving our presents to poor Ly. Lyttelton, a bracelet containing the portraits of our five younger Children, & 2 prints of the Children. Then gave presents to our personal servants &c, & were busy arranging the tables.

At a little after 6 we all assembled & my beloved Albert 1rst took me to my tree & table, covered by such numberless gifts, really too much, too magnificent. I am delighted with the really splendid picture in watercolours by Corbauld, representing the famous scene at the Coronation in 'Le Prophète' – & a very pretty oil painting of 'Faith' represented by a female figure & 2 angels, by Mrs. Richards, also a fine oil painting of 'L'Allegro' & 'Il Penseroso', by Hurseley. The one present from dearest Albert, which is of infinite value to me, is a miniature of my beloved Louise in a clasp to a bracelet in dull, deepish blue enamel, with a black cross, the cypher & stars in diamonds, all, dear Albert's own design & very lovely.

I also received charming gifts from dear Mama. The 3 girls all worked me something. The 7 children were then taken to their tree, jumping & shouting with joy over their toys & other presents; the Boys could think of nothing but the swords we had given them, & Bertie of some armour, which however he complained, pinched him!

Mama had her tree & table in the same room, & Albert his, in the 3rd last room. Amongst my gifts was a painting by Landseer, as a pendant to his 'Lassie' – a Highlander in a snowstorm 'on the Hull', with a dead eagle in one hand, & a dog near him. The colouring is beautiful, & the whole thing is a 'chef d'oeuvre'.

Dear Albert was kindly pleased with everything, but I felt it was so poor in comparison to what he had given me. At 7, we gave the Ladies & Gentlemen their tree and gifts, & then showed them our things. Mama, &c to dinner, Ld. Camoys sitting next to me, having just come into waiting . . .

25th December 1850. Windsor Castle.
The return of this blessed season must always fill one with gratitude & with the deepest devotion to Our Lord &

Queen Victoria driving at Windsor in the winter of 1894, attended
by her Highland attendant Francis Clark. This early photograph is
attributed to Princess Victoria of Wales

Saviour! May God grant that we may all see many happy
returns of this great Festival. We walked with the Children
to the Kennels, where I gave the good little McDonalds toys
& stuff for dresses. The day was beautiful but almost too
mild for Christmas! Service at 11. Went several times to look

at my beautiful presents. The trees were lit up in the evening, & the Children were all playing about so happily. Mama, &c – the Phippses, Mrs. Grey, Mrs. Bouverie, Gen. Wemyss, Mr. Wellesley, Mr. Birch, Mr. Glover & Meyer, dined. The 2 little girls & Affie appeared during dinner, & the others, after.

26th December 1850. Windsor Castle.

A dull & raw morning. Albert, out hunting, & I, walking with the Children. The little McDonalds & little Flemmings (to whom I had also given something) were much delighted with their Xmas presents, when we went in to see them. Rode afterwards in the Riding School on 'Hammon' & 'Ronald'. A rainy afternoon, but got out for a short walk. At ½ p. 6 the Children performed their Charade, the same as last year, but without the dancing & the last scene. Some of the scenery from our Theatre was made use of, & the whole looked very nice. The Children were particularly well got up, but did not act as well, being rather absent. Bertie spoke the best. They each recited a piece of poetry, and Bertie the 7 Ages, by Shakespeare, which he did remarkably well. The performance ended with a little dance with the Phipps Children, who had come to see the Charade. Bessy Douro, Caroline Cavendish, Stockmar, & Clark were also there. Mama, &c to dinner.

The Wind Across the Wild Moor

TRADITIONAL

In this the second example of the traditional verses collected early this century by Alfred Williams in Folk Songs of the Upper Thames, *the subject is the rejection of a mother's plea for shelter for herself and her child on a bitter winter's night.*
Perhaps because it has one or two similarities with the Christmas story – not least the name Mary – this poignant ballad, dating from the early 1800s, would have been popular during the festive season in many an old Berkshire inn, with the log fire blazing to keep out the cold.

'Twas one cold winter's night, and the wind
Blew bitter across the wild moor,
'Twas then Mary went with her child,
Wandering home to her own father's door,
Crying, 'Father, I pray, let me in;
Oh, come down and open the door,
Or the child at my bosom will die
With the wind that blows across the wild moor.

'Oh, why did I leave that fair spot,
Where I was happy and free,
For ever to roam, without friend or home?
Pray, father, take pity on me.'

But he was deaf to the cry,
When the sound reached him over the door;
The watchdogs barked, and the wind
Blew bitter across the wild moor.

You can't think what a father he felt
When he came to the door in the morn;
He found Mary dead, but the child
Clasped alive in a dead mother's arm.
With vengeance he tore his grey hair,
On his Mary he gazed from the door;
'Twas in that cold night she perished and died
By the wind that blew across the wild moor.

The father in grief pined away,
And the child to its mother went soon,
There's no-one lives there to this day,
The cottage to ruins is gone;
The villager points out the cot
Where the wild rose droops over the door,
'Twas there Mary died, by the house of her pride,
With the wind that blew across the wild moor.

from

Travels Round Our Village

ELEANOR G. HAYDEN

Eleanor Hayden's delightful book, published in the last year of Victoria's reign, is a perceptive and entertaining account of life at that time in a small rural community near Wantage, long before this part of Berkshire was engulfed by neighbouring Oxfordshire, following the boundary changes of modern times. She describes the village as 'a quiet backwater such as may yet be found in rural England, which the tide of progress stirs but just enough to avert stagnation'. In the following extract the author introduces us to two of the village characters – Farmer Pinmarsh and his wife – and offers us a fascinating insight into the annual ritual surrounding the preparation of festive fare at Christmastime. The extract opens with a few of Farmer Pinmarsh's more caustic comments on the 'threats' to Britain's traditional agriculture posed by new working practices and free-trade legislation, which were having their effect around the turn of the century.

Being no less old-fashioned than his wife, the farmer strongly condemns free trade which he holds is ruining England and draining her of money to enrich aliens.

'Why,' he asks, 'cannot the foreigner keep his nasty food in his own country? We should do a deal better without it over here. If folks would be content with wholesome home-grown stuff they wouldn't get half the bad diseases they do . . . You don't know what you are eating nowadays, and farming is just being throttled by everything coming in free! The wonder is enough fools can be found to take the land, seeing every year we've more difficulty in making a living out of it.'

Notwithstanding these vaticinations, Farmer Pinmarsh, with others as shrewd and industrious as himself, continues to lay by a trifle, and to lack meanwhile none of the necessaries and few of the comforts of life. Nevertheless it is true that large fortunes can no longer be made by farming, and the last thirty years which have brought the labourer prosperity, his master has found lean.

With them have departed much of the proverbial farmhouse abundance; this is seen now only on special occasions – as at Christmas – when scattered families unite beneath the paternal roof. Then indeed, the board groans under the weight of good cheer; the turkey or fowls reserved to that purpose when the remainder were sold, will be sacrificed; cakes and pies will overflow from the farm oven to the village bakehouse, and one of the mighty hams, weighing forty pounds and upwards, will be unslung from its hook and boiled – in the copper because the house contains no vessel large enough to hold it.

Very excellent eating these hams are, rivalling if not excelling those of Yorkshire justly famed. In fact, the best I have ever tasted was cured by the following recipe:

'When the weather permits, hang the ham three days; mix 1 oz of saltpetre, ¼ lb of bay salt, the same quantity of common salt and of coarse sugar, with two quarts of strong beer. Boil them all together and turn immediately upon the ham. If the latter be so large that the pickle seems inadequate, double the quantity of beer. Turn the ham in the pickle twice a day for

Winter snow mantles the farming countryside near Wantage, the
setting for Eleanor Hayden's book

three weeks. 1 oz of black pepper and the same amount of
allspice in fine powder added to the above will give it still more
flavour. Cover the ham, when wiped, with bran, and smoke
from three to four weeks as you approve. The latter period will
make it harder and give it more the flavour of Westphalian
hams. These ingredients are only sufficient for one ham; if two
are to be cured, double the quantities. If smoked by a strong
fire, the ham should be sewn in coarse wrappering.'

Mrs Pinmarsh possesses some curious ancient recipes (of
which she allowed me to copy a few) that have been handed
down in her family for several generations. That given below
for Christmas pudding – in modern terms for the convenience
of my readers – she knows to be at least two hundred years
old. It came to her from her great-aunt who died at the
advanced age of ninety-three, and the latter in her turn
received it from her grandmother:

'2 lbs of raisins, stoned; 2 lbs of currants; 2 lbs of suet; 1½ lbs of flour; ½ lb of breadcrumbs; 2¾ lbs of sugar; ¼ lb of chopped candied peel; 8 eggs; and 1 quart of milk. Mix all the ingredients together and let them stand during the night in order to swell the bread. Then if too stiff, add a little more milk. Turn in a glass of brandy and boil for four hours, and one hour before sending to the table.'

In making the above, it should be remembered, as the farmer's wife pointed out to me, that in old days a pudding of this description would probably be boiled in a cloth and would therefore require a shorter period than one boiled in a mould. She allows at least eight hours, being well aware, good housekeeper as she is, that a plum pudding's excellence depends scarcely less on the manner and time of its cooking, than on the material of which it is made.

This fact was amusingly demonstrated at the Diamond Jubilee. We celebrated it by a gala day in which a public dinner played an important part according to the orthodox English fashion. The Christmas puddings were entrusted to the various better-class housewives of the village, who were each supplied with an equal amount of raw material. When the manufactured articles were marshalled ready for the table, it was seen that they ranged in colour from light fawn to a rich brown that was almost black. There was no urgent demand for the pale uninviting-looking dumplings, and the chagrined makers broke forth into indignant remonstrances, declaring that the original ingredients of the others must have been largely supplemented to have produced such different results. They could with difficulty be persuaded that these were solely due to more lengthened periods of boiling . . .

Years ago, ere the sons and daughters left their father's roof for homes of their own, and when agriculture was more lucrative than at present, the Pinmarshs' farm was the scene

of many jovial gatherings. At Christmas high revel was held.

The lasses and lads from neighbouring farms were bidden, and arrived amid the darkness of the winter evening, the former resplendent in best bib and tucker, the latter awkwardly conscious of Sunday clothes, with hair and faces shining from recent ablutions.

A solemn stiffness befitting the little-used apartment pervaded the company when it assembled in the best parlour. The men clung bashfully together near the fireplace, exchanging remarks upon the weather, the state of the crops, the prospects of the lambing season, in voices rendered husky by damp and shyness; the girls, demure and self-possessed, sat in a semi-circle round the room conversing with decorous primness on equally absorbing topics of a domestic nature.

The announcement that supper was ready, caused a visible thaw. Henceforth the business of the evening would be conducted on well-defined lines; each guest knew what would be expected of him or her, the first duty being the consumption of as large a part as possible of the viands prepared.

The meal, overpowering in its abundance to one whose appetite had not been previously sharpened by country air and exercise, was spread in the kitchen, which was decorated with holly and evergreens. Above the centre of the table depended a large bunch of mistletoe, and this by pointing many a jest and furnishing the theme for divers sly allusions, served as an effective aid to conversation.

Supper banished shyness, loosened the most unready tongue, and set laughter free until the black-beamed ceiling rang again. But it was when the feast was ended, and the table was pushed into one corner, that the real fun began.

In those days healthy young men and maidens left cards to

their elders; such energetic pastimes as country dances, blind man's buff and hunt the slipper accorded better with their simple active life. Their mirth though noisy was innocent, and if a kiss or two were snatched beneath the mistletoe during the hurly-burly, the offence as a rule was speedily condoned by the insulted damsel, who accepted the reasonableness of her swain's argument that it would be 'nothen but a waste fur Farmer Pinmarsh to hang up that fine bough if no use weren't made on it'.

Two ceremonies interrupted the games, and gave the players time to restore exhausted nature. The first was the appearance of a flaming bowl of snapdragon which elicited shrieks from the girls, and provoked the lads to deeds of daring in the struggle for the largest number of raisins, these being subsequently offered on Cupid's altar by each youth to his own bright particular star.

The second interruption was the arrival of the Mummers – King George, the Doctor, white horse and all – of whom a poor remnant still survives in the village. They regularly received a previous hint from the farmer that they would be welcomed on these occasions, and as regularly expressed their regret at intruding when 'Maister had got comp'ny', which little piece of politeness was considered an essential part of the programme.

The party broke up in the small hours of the morning, and departed to their various homes, after partaking of hot punch brewed by Mr Pinmarsh as he sat in his armchair watching the young folks.

In a later chapter, Eleanor Hayden delves again into an old book of seasonal recipes which she and her sister 'unearthed from a lumber-chest in an attic at the Manor'.

The book originally belonged to the grandmother of a dear

old friend of our childhood and contains directions for every imaginable culinary contingency, from roasting a plain joint to making muffins. One Richard Briggs compiled it, who was for many years cook at various taverns in London. Aware of the difficulty of his task, he submits it with 'deference and respect, conscious that errors will creep into the best performance, and that the only merit I can claim is that of having corrected the mistakes of former works, and added the most useful improvements derived from my own practice and experience'.

The following 'Common Plumb Porridge for Christmas' combines quality with quantity in a manner quite after Master Briggs' heart.

'Take a leg and shin of beef and cut them small and put them into eight gallons of water. When the scum rises, skim it well. Boil for six hours, then strain it into a pan. Clean out the pot and pour your broth in again. Slice the crumb of six

Mrs Pinmarsh makes her Christmas pudding – an illustration from *Travels Round Our Village*

penny loaves very thin, and put some of the broth to them.
Cover them up for a quarter of an hour and then give it a boil
up and rub it through a sieve. Have ready six pounds of
currants well washed and picked, four pounds of jar raisins
picked and stoned, and two pounds of pruens. Boil all these in
the soup till they swell and are tender, then put in half an
ounce of mace, half an ounce of cloves and two nutmegs, all
beat fine. Mix them in a little cold broth first, and then put
them in with four pounds of sugar, two quarts of sack, and the
juice of four lemons. Boil it up ten minutes, keep it stirring,
then put it into earthen pans and put it by for use. When you
want it, make it hot and send it in a soup dish or tureen with
crispt French bread.'

Mr Briggs' imagination does not soar to any great heights on
the subject of puddings. He has no fewer than seven preparations
of rice all very much alike, and six of bread. Among the recipes
for pies, of which the book contains a goodly number, are
directions for a 'Swan Pie' that recall those sets of Indian boxes
packed one inside another. First you take a fowl, stuff it with veal
and bacon and lay it in the breast of a goose. This again is to be
inserted in the swan, which is then to be placed in a dish, covered
with crust and surmounted by a swan modelled in butter; or
should the cook be unequal to the creation of this work of art, by
a wax model which can be purchased.

'There is a great deal of work in this dish,' concludes the
author plaintively.

'Yorkshire Pie for Christmas' is very like the foregoing,
except that it contains an even larger number of 'boxes',
which include a turkey, a goose, a large fowl, a partridge and a
pigeon, all fitting one inside the other. It might reasonably
have been supposed that these were sufficient for one dish; but
no such thing! A hare, six woodcock, some moor-game or
small wild-fowl are to be laid around the turkey, and the
whole is to be enclosed within ramparts of crust, for which a

bushel of flour and ten pounds of butter are directed to be used.

It is significant that at the end of his book, Mr Briggs gives a recipe for 'Surfeit Water', and that among the herbs from which it is distilled, rue and wormwood find a prominent place!

from

Letters to Cassandra Austen

JANE AUSTEN

Jane Austen, one of the most celebrated novelists of English literary history, lived from 1775 to 1817. Her father, the Reverend George Austen, was the rector of the adjoining parishes of Steventon and Deane, over the Hampshire border near Basingstoke, and although much of her life was spent at Steventon Rectory, she could also justly claim numerous associations with Berkshire and its borderlands. She was educated in Reading, at an establishment located in the gatehouse of Reading Abbey which was a forerunner of the town's present-day Abbey School. A nephew, J.E. Austen-Leigh, was the vicar of Bray; an aunt was married to a Dr Cooper,

vicar of the Thames-side village of Sonning near Reading; and her maternal grandfather, the Reverend Thomas Leigh, held the living at Harpsden, close to Berkshire's border with Oxfordshire. She also had connections with the Berkshire village of Kintbury where she stayed occasionally at the family home of the fiancé of her elder sister Cassandra. The two sisters had always been extremely close during childhood and adolescence, and when family circumstances later demanded frequent separations, they regularly exchanged letters, often twice a week, in order to keep each other informed of the day-to-day happenings which influenced their respective lives. Jane's letters to Cassandra are especially revealing. Not only do they reflect her innate ability as a descriptive writer, but through the fascinating minutiae of their content, they shed a revealing light on the social attitudes which governed middle-class life in the late eighteenth century. The following example, which is slightly abridged, was written to Cassandra on the night of Christmas Eve in 1798. Strangely perhaps, it makes no direct reference to the festive season, or to the fact that Christmas Day itself was only an hour or so away, but concentrates instead on the sort of social detail with which the two sisters were happily preoccupied. The ball which is mentioned, however, was presumably a pre-Christmas party, and the gifts to charities to which Jane refers were no doubt a seasonal gesture. The various named guests at the ball were family friends and neighbours.

Monday night, December 24th

My Dear Cassandra,

Our ball was very thin, but by no means unpleasant. There were thirty-one people, and only eleven ladies out of the number, and but five single women in the room. Of the gentlemen present you may have some idea from the list of my partners – Mr Wood, G. Lefroy, Rice, a Mr Butcher (belonging

An original portrait of Jane
Austen by her sister
Cassandra

to the Temples, a sailor and not of the 11th Light Dragoons),
Mr Temple (not the horrid one of all), Mr Wm Orde (cousin to
the Kingsclere man), Mr John Harwood, and Mr Calland who
appeared as usual with his hat in his hand, and stood every now
and then behind Catherine and me to be talked to and abused
for not dancing. We teased him, however, into it at last. I was
very glad to see him again after so long a separation . . .

There were twenty dances and I danced them all without any
fatigue . . . My black cap was openly admired by Mrs Lefroy,
and secretly I imagine by everybody else in the room . . .

Of my charities to the poor since I came home you shall
have a faithful account. I have given a pair of worsted
stockings to Mary Hutchins, Dame Kew, Mary Steevens and
Dame Staples; a shift to Hannah Staples, and a shawl to Betty
Dawkins; amounting in all to about half a guinea . . .

I was to have dined at Deane today, but the weather is so
cold that I am not sorry to be kept at home by the appearance

of snow. We are to have company to dinner on Friday: the three Digweeds and James. We shall be a nice silent party, I suppose.

You deserve a longer letter than this; but it is my unhappy fate seldom to treat people so well as they deserve . . . God bless you!

Yours affectionately,
Jane Austen

Curiously Jane signed her letters to Cassandra in a variety of ways, frequently – as here – using her full name in formal fashion. At other times she would abbreviate it to 'J. Austen' or 'J.A.', only occasionally signing the single name 'Jane'.

from
Sunday Chimes
HENRY GODWIN

In 1866, the poet Henry Godwin, who lived at Speen Hill near Newbury, produced an anthology of his poetry under the title Sunday Chimes. *His work reflected his thoughts on a wide range of subjects, often revealing his deeply held religious convictions, as in the following verses which he called 'Christmas Day'.*

Hush'd was the sound of war,
The long vex'd earth had rest,
Save that the city's hum afar
Rose like the breathings of a child distrest,
That sobs itself to sleep upon its mother's breast.

Softly the moon look'd down,
As pitying mortals frail;
On Olive's glistening summit shone,
With holy Jordan communed in the vale,
And o'er the Dead Sea hung, to view her image pale.

Sleep wrapt the weary world,
Save where, in studious mood,
The sage his mystic scroll unfurl'd,
Or on lone tower the seer star-watching stood,
Or shepherds with light song their drowsiness subdued.

Suddenly, angel-strains
Peal'd through the midnight sky;
And, lighting soft on Judah's plains,
A choir of radiant minstrels from on high,
With light and music fill'd Heaven's purple canopy!

'Glory to God on high!'
Sweetly the lay began;
Then, as the echoes found reply,
It rose, till 'Peace on earth, goodwill to man',
In one seraphic swell, along the mountains ran.

'Good tidings of great joy,
Shepherds, to you we bring;
Let holier themes your songs employ;
This day is born a Saviour and a King;
Arise, to Bethlehem haste, Hosannas there to sing.'

'Glory to God on high!'
Once more burst forth the strain,
As 'twould dissolve the echoing sky;
One blaze of starlight glory fill'd the plain,
And then the squadron bright to Heaven return'd again.

Messiah shone reveal'd
On scroll but erst so dim;
Chaldaea's seer, with eyes unseal'd,
Beheld the new-lit star of Bethlehem;
The shepherds hail'd the babe adored by Seraphim.

Glory to God on high!
We too may learn the lay:
When every star shall quit the sky,
And, like a shrivell'd scroll, heaven pass away,
Thou, Lord, shalt but commence Thy never-ending
   sway!

Immortal Prince of peace!
Vouchsafe this boon divine;
'When Thou shalt reign in righteousness,
Oh, grant that we, whose nature Thou mad'st Thine,
Regenerate, and renew'd, may in Thine image shine!'

Ghosts Galore

CHARLES CUNNINGHAM

The Christmas season has always been a favourite time for relating tales of the supernatural. A yule log blazing in the hearth, and the winter wind howling in the chimney and buffeting the doors and windows: what better setting for a few spine-chilling stories? Even in our modern homes, when impersonal central heating has so often usurped the time-honoured role of the open fire, the ghost story tradition still survives, now perpetuated more often than not by radio and television. Berkshire and its borderlands can boast their fair share of supernatural occurrences spanning many centuries, as writer Charles Cunningham discovered when he delved into the area's spectral past.

In and around Berkshire, ghostly tales abound. Some of them recall incidents of undisguised horror, others are shrouded in sorrow; a few even have an amusing aspect, especially to those of a sceptical disposition who tend to regard anything to do with the supernatural with a firmly raised eyebrow.

But the stories persist, handed down from generation to generation, occasionally strengthened by what the believers see as fresh evidence or a new slant on interpretation. Can these tales, some of which are associated with irrefutable historical fact, really be dismissed as nothing more than a figment of the imagination?

Take the ghost which is said to haunt historic Bisham Abbey near Maidenhead. According to all the evidence, it

appears in the form of a woman dressed in white, thought to be Lady Hoby who lived in the abbey in the sixteenth century. She was a scholarly woman, proficient in Greek and Latin, who became increasingly intolerant of her eldest son due to his complete disinterest in learning. Every page the boy wrote in his school books was covered in blots and almost illegible because of his untidy handwriting.

One day, Lady Hoby could control herself no longer, and in a sudden fit of anger she beat the unfortunate boy to death. The story might well have ended there and been handed down as an apocryphal legend, but for a chance discovery made by workmen in the last century while they were undertaking repairs in the old abbey. Beneath the floorboards they discovered a number of early school books, and they contained not a single line without blots.

It would seem that Lady Hoby subsequently regretted the dreadful punishment she gave her son, and her repentant ghost has returned to the scene of the crime ever since. Her face is shrouded in sorrow, and she constantly washes her hands in a bowl which floats before her, in apparent atonement for her sin.

Another of Berkshire's ghostly ladies, this one a good deal more benevolent than the impulsive Lady Hoby, is said to have frequented the old rectory at Yattendon to the west of Reading, for some twenty years in the early part of the present century.

She was a shadowy but friendly figure in eighteenth-century dress, known affectionately to the rector and his family as 'Mrs It', and favouring the former servants' quarters for her wanderings. She was certain to appear during the festive season, and would often visit the kitchen while the rector's wife was preparing the Christmas dinner. Because of her interest in this part of the old house, the belief arose that 'Mrs It' was once a housekeeper there, or at least a member of the household staff.

When the rector and his family moved on to a new parish, 'Mrs It' apparently ceased her visitations, unless of course she still lurks unseen in the rectory corridors when the spirit of Christmas is in the air.

Not far from the rectory at Yattendon lies the village of Basildon, scene of another haunting by a Berkshire ghost. This time, the apparition is of a seventeenth-century wheelwright mounted on a white horse, who seems to favour the long winter nights for his appearances. He was, according to local legend, something of a miser, and before he died he gave instructions that all his money should be buried with him and that the key to his cottage should be dropped into his tomb through a special hole cut in the roof for the purpose.

Whether or not his last wishes were ever carried out is not recorded, but local folk have vouched for the fact that slow footsteps have been heard ascending from the tomb at night, when the old miserly wheelwright has emerged on his trusty steed. Why he should have done this remains a mystery, unless he has been vainly searching for his money and his key, which perhaps were not actually placed in his tomb as he had instructed.

Not surprisingly, many of the old mansions in and around Berkshire have their own ghost stories to tell, not the least of which is the historic red-brick manor house at Mapledurham by the side of the Thames on the county's border with Oxfordshire. Built in Elizabethan times by the Blount family, this fine old house is still occupied by their descendants to this day. It contains numerous secret hiding places from the days of religious persecution, and there are many stories of ghostly happenings associated with the bloodshed and tragedy of those turbulent times.

One such tale mentions the skeleton of a Cavalier, discovered behind wall panelling, who is said to be the same proud soldier who supposedly appears in the house from time

The Elizabethan manor house at Mapledurham is the setting for
many stories of ghostly happenings

to time, perhaps still seeking revenge on his killer. Another
story talks of the ghost of a former servant, killed by the
sword of an Elizabethan nobleman, who has allegedly been
seen walking abroad in the building he once knew so well.

Yet another of Mapledurham's ghostly sightings is that of a
spectral cleric who at certain times has been observed
wandering in the old house. Some say he was an unfortunate
priest who was drowned in the Thames while trying to escape
persecution, and that on each anniversary of his death, he
emerges from the river and makes his way to the manor
chapel. Here, in these more enlightened times, he no doubt
finds brief peace without fear.

Such stories inevitably become blurred over the years, and
are often confused with other similar tales of the supernatural.
This could be why an alternative explanation of the ghostly
cleric identifies him not as a recusant priest, but as a
nineteenth-century vicar of Mapledurham.

It seems that on one dark winter evening, the good vicar was due to preach in the neighbouring parish of Purley on the opposite bank of the Thames. He set off to cross the river by boat but apparantly failed to reach the other side. He was never seen or heard of again, although his ghost evidently lives on, the spectral custodian of the sermon that was never preached

But whether persecuted priest or vanished vicar, Mapledurham's clerical ghost is benign enough, and certainly poses no threat if you should ever encounter him.

And if you happen to be out and about in the lanes of Mapledurham on a winter's night, when a cold wind argues with the bare trees and stirs the restless waters of the river, you may well hear the rattle of wheels and the sound of horses' hooves echoing in the darkness. These are said to belong to a phantom hearse pulled by four black horses, making its way at midnight to some unknown destination.

Berkshire and its borderlands can also boast what is said to be one of the five most haunted houses in England. This is Littlecote, the home of entrepreneur and businessman Peter de Savary, not far from Hungerford by Berkshire's border with Wiltshire. With as many as twenty ghosts to its name, this magnificent old house was built by the Darrell family in the fifteenth and early sixteenth centuries, and it was one of the Darrells who committed a deed in 1575 which gave rise to Littlecote's most macabre and enduring ghost story.

Known as 'Wild' Will Darrell, he was said to have murdered a newborn baby in the house by throwing it on to a blazing fire and holding it there with his boot until it was dead.

The story came to light some fourteen years later when the midwife who had been present at the baby's birth reported the facts to a magistrate. By now elderly and approaching the end of her life, she confessed that although she had been bribed to keep her mouth shut, she felt she could conceal the facts no

Littlecote near Hungerford, reputed to be one of the five most
haunted houses in England

longer. She maintained that the baby's mother, who had been
forcibly masked at the time of the crime so that she could not
witness it, was in fact Darrell's own sister who had become
pregnant by Darrell himself.

Darrell was duly brought to trial and engaged his cousin,
Sir John Popham, to defend him. Popham happened to be
Attorney General at the time, and perhaps it was no
coincidence that after Darrell was acquitted of the murder,
Popham was bequeathed the Littlecote estate in Darrell's will.

Darrell had seemingly got away with his heinous crime,
but retribution was not long delayed. A few years later while
he was riding on his estate, he was suddenly confronted by the
ghost of the baby he had killed. His horse shied in terror, and
Darrell was thrown to the ground, breaking his neck.

One of the bedrooms at Littlecote. Conjecture surrounds the ghostly apparition beyond the four-poster bed – could it be the figure of a sixteenth-century midwife who witnessed a foul murder, or is it the mother of a baby which met its death in 1862?

There are some who have refused to accept the story, suggesting that it is more likely Darrell was killed on Popham's instructions to hasten the inheritance of the estate. Be that as it may, it remains a fact that even today, more than 400 years later, horses are still said to shy at this same spot.

Another of Littlecote's many ghost stories relates to an incident which occurred as recently as 1985, and it was witnessed by Peter de Savary himself. Strangely, like the story of 'Wild' Will Darrell, it also involves a baby.

It was at about 9.30 one morning, and Peter de Savary was walking along a servants' corridor in the house when he was

suddenly confronted by a well-dressed lady in present-day costume, probably in her forties. He had never seen her before, but was not particularly surprised as there were one or two strangers around at the time, connected with the sale of some of the contents of the house later that day.

He therefore greeted her courteously, but instead of replying, the woman menacingly accused him of having moved her baby's clothes from the place where she had left them, and that he and his family would suffer unless they were put back.

Thinking she was referring to some minor incident possibly concerned with the forthcoming sale, he assured the woman he would look into the matter and have the clothes returned to her immediately. But this did not seem to satisfy her, and subjecting him to a fixed stare, she said he did not understand and that she herself could not have the clothes anyway.

He now assumed he was speaking to someone who was either wildly eccentric or whose mind was disturbed, so to placate the woman he agreed to find the clothes by following her instructions and to put them back in the place where she said she had left them. With that, the woman smiled, assured him that he and his family would now live in the house happily, and then just disappeared as if she had evaporated into thin air.

It was only then that Peter de Savary realised with some horror that he had encountered a ghost, and in a state of considerable shock went to find his wife to report what had happened. Insisting that the planned furniture sale could not now be allowed to start until the clothes had been found, they set about searching for them. The clothes were eventually discovered, and with them was a baby's hand-brush and a poignant note apparently written by the mother at the time of the baby's death – in 1862.

In the private chapel at Littlecote is a tiny effigy of a baby – the same child whose clothes Peter de Savary had found and whose mother he had encountered in such strange circumstances.

Ghosts of the more distant past are also said to inhabit Littlecote and its environs, as a group of archaeologists discovered during the excavation of the remains of a nearby Roman villa. While these perfectly rational scientists were working on the site, they became aware of the sound of Roman soldiers marching along the old Roman road which passes close by. It was not a phenomenon experienced by just one person. They all heard it, and were able to describe the clanking of heavy armour and the rhythmic tramping of feet, growing louder as the soldiers approached, and then diminishing as they marched away into the distance.

There have been nocturnal sightings, too, of a darkly robed monk-like figure among the trees on the estate, while the guides who conduct visitors round the house have frequently reported having their hair or clothing mysteriously tugged when there has been no-one in sight.

It's small wonder that Littlecote has acquired its reputation for the supernatural, but on the whole the ghosts which share this fascinating old house with Peter de Savary and his family are a benign lot, and pose no threat to anyone provided they are left alone.

Littlecote's robed monk is not the only apparition of this description which is reputed to have haunted Berkshire on dark winter nights. Back in the seventeenth century, long before the modern main road was built between Reading and Basingstoke, the track linking the two towns passed close to a bleak hilltop site known as Catern's Grave. Even then, mystery surrounded the origin of the place, and no-one knew for sure who Catern was and why he should have been buried in so remote a spot.

But his secrets were closely guarded, and anyone who was unwise enough to venture too close to the hilltop would be confronted by a terrifying hooded monk who would appear from a clump of fir trees nearby. On other occasions, it was said that a whole band of these menacing apparitions would challenge intruders and drive them away with brandished stakes.

The fact that ghostly monks were the guardians of the grave, gave rise to the legend that Catern may well have been one of their number, a holy man whose last resting place was never to be disturbed. Whatever the truth of the story, those who wander that way at night, even today, would do well to watch out for the dark figures of hooded monks hiding in the shadows.

The sound of phantom carriage wheels and galloping horses is not an uncommon phenomenon in many parts of the country, and Berkshire can claim numerous such incidents, especially on frosty winter nights. At Swallowfield, just to the south of Reading, the ghostly sound of chariot wheels and horses' hooves has apparently often been heard along an old road built by the Romans which became known as the Devil's Highway.

A few miles to the north-west at Bucklebury near Thatcham, there have been reports of a phantom carriage drawn by four black horses, urged on by headless riders. The occupant of the carriage, a lady dressed in white, is said to be the beautiful Frances, daughter of Sir Henry Winchcombe of Bucklebury, who married Henry St John, 1st Viscount Bolingbroke. She died in 1718, apparently from a broken heart, and the ghostly carriage journeys she has undertaken ever since, are said to be taking her back to Bucklebury's Elizabethan manor house which had been her family home.

Not surprisingly, many of Berkshire's more prestigious ghosts reside at the historic royal home of Windsor Castle, where no less than four former monarchs, apart from a

number of lesser individuals, are said to manifest themselves in spectral form when the winter nights are dark and the wind howls around the ancient towers.

Henry VIII, for instance, can sometimes be distinctly heard, shuffling and wheezing, as he drags his painful ulcerated leg along one of the corridors. Elizabeth I, dressed in black and wearing a black lace head-scarf, has been seen as well as heard. One such sighting was apparently made by a Lieutenant Glynn of the Grenadier Guards in 1897 while he was reading in the royal library. His account was evidently corroborated by one of the castle servants who reported that the Tudor queen had, in fact, been seen in the library on a number of occasions, when the sound of her footsteps on the polished floor could clearly be detected.

Charles I is another of the castle's royal ghosts, and although a number of personages who were beheaded are said to reappear here in their decapitated state, the body of this particular monarch apparently manifests itself in its entirety, the face closely resembling the likeness portrayed in so many paintings.

The fourth former monarch reputed to haunt Windsor's historic castle is the unfortunate George III, whose life was marred by periods of madness. Many seemingly reliable observers, including officials of the royal household, are said to have encountered the ghost of the king who died at the castle in 1820.

Towards the end of his life he spent much of his time under restraint in his apartment, playing on his harpsichord when he was not ranting at his staff. The sounds of his voice and his music have both been heard, and on one occasion he is said to have been seen at a window returning a salute to the captain of the royal guard.

But royal spectres apart, Windsor's best-known ghost must be that of the legendary Herne the Hunter who once roamed

Windsor Forest and is still said to have been sighted from time to time in the Great Park. He makes his appearances mounted on a ghostly black steed and his head sprouts the antlers of a stag.

The story, of which there are several versions, probably owes its existence to the mythology of pagan times, when it was customary to dress up as wild beasts as part of a seasonal ritual held around the winter solstice.

More popularly it is said to date back to the reign of Richard II when Herne was a keeper in the forest. One day, during a royal hunt, a wounded stag turned on the king who would have died if Herne had not slaughtered the enraged beast with his knife. The hunter, too, was injured, but a

A nineteenth-century depiction of Herne the Hunter on his black steed confronting Henry VIII in Windsor Forest. Windsor Castle rises above the trees in the background

magician who lived in the forest was permitted by the king to effect a cure which entailed fixing the dead stag's antlers to Herne's own head.

But after Herne's recovery, the king's gratitude did not last long. Following several unsuccessful days of hunting, the monarch dismissed Herne in a fit of rage, and the unfortunate hunter, overcome by disgrace, hanged himself on the branch of an oak tree.

This same tree, known as Herne's Oak, survived until 1863 when, according to some sources it blew down in a gale. Other reports say that Queen Victoria ordered it to be felled following complaints from her tenants who were frightened by its historical association with the ghostly Herne.

Whichever version of the story is correct, it seems that Queen Victoria had a replacement sapling planted in the old oak's place, and that the antlered hunter, mounted on his spectral steed and with hunting horn at his lips, still visits the same spot during his demoniacal excursions in what was once the royal forest he knew so well.

This has always been one of Windsor's great tales of the supernatural, immortalised by Harrison Ainsworth in his stirring historical novel *Windsor Castle*. Herne, 'the foul fiend of the forest', makes numerous dramatic appearances during the course of the story, and on one such occasion he haunts Henry VIII and upbraids the monarch for plotting the death of the hapless Anne Boleyn in favour of Jane Seymour.

Shakespeare, too, was familiar with the legend of Herne the Hunter, as Mistress Anne Page quotes it in *The Merry Wives of Windsor*:

> There is an old tale goes that Herne the Hunter,
> Sometime a keeper here in Windsor Forest,
> Doth all the winter-time, at still midnight,
> Walk round about an oak, with great ragg'd horns;

And there he blasts the tree, and takes the cattle,
And makes milch-kine yield blood, and shakes a chain
In a most hideous and dreadful manner.
You have heard of such a spirit, and well you know
The superstitious idle-headed eld
Received and did deliver to our age
This tale of Herne the Hunter for a truth.

The epic tale is well worth relating, along with all those other stories of Berkshire ghosts, when the nights are dark and the Christmas spirit flows freely.

from

My Own Trumpet

DION CLAYTON CALTHROP

Under the heading 'Christmas Jottings', the 1935 Christmas issue of Reading Review *chose extracts from* My Own Trumpet *as a timely contribution to its coverage of the festive season that year. The book is the autobiography of the artist, author and playwright Dion Clayton Calthrop, who died two years later. These evocative Christmas reminiscences from his late-Victorian childhood belong to the period shortly after his father's death when he and his sister were placed in the guardianship of an uncle.*

My most poignant memory of this time is of my first Christmas Day in my uncle's house. Full of expectancy I came down to breakfast with my sister. There were no letters for me, no parcels. My uncle came down and I wished him a Happy Christmas. That was all that happened. He had remembered the servants, remembered his tenant farmers, his sisters, his mother, but we two Babes in the Wood he had forgotten.

We went to church, I at least with my heart in my boots, but it was cheerful to see people with faces rosy with the cold, stamping the snow off their boots in the porch, to hear the Christmas hymns and see the decorations.

In our absence my uncle had worked miracles. There was holly and mistletoe over the pictures in the dining room, and by our plates was a present for each of us. I remember mine well. It was a large silver pencil such as an important person might bring out in order to write notes in court.

There was no Christmas fare for lunch, but I knew from my friend the cook, who had the odd name of Fermado, that a real Christmas dinner was in preparation for six o'clock.

Long before six the special dessert was placed ready outside the dining room door; apples, winter pears which tasted slightly of wood and straw, almonds and raisins, Brazil nuts, crab apple cheese, ginger, and preserved red and white currants.

It was a gargantuan feast with the largest turkey I had ever seen, with plum pudding alight with brandy, mince pies and Stilton cheese. We were given a glass of champagne which my sister sipped at and sneezed violently as the bubbles went up her nose, and we stuffed ourselves with food.

Then came dessert and a glass of port and a health. This completely bowled my sister over, and she fell asleep over the table, and was carried to bed. To top up this extraordinary evening my uncle read aloud to me 'The Jackdaw of Rheims' from the Ingoldsby Legends during which I think I too must have fallen asleep.

Dion Clayton Calthrop,
photographed in the 1930s

Next morning, however, everything was altered. The London mail had been held up by snowdrifts and our letters and parcels had been delayed. Presents and letters arrived from those of my father's friends who knew where we were, and I could have hugged the world and especially the extra postman who delivered a piece of my old life at the door . . .

I had a toy theatre on the proscenium of which was painted my full name as sole lessee and manager: Dion William Palgrave Clayton Calthrop. My grandfather had made it for me and wrote some of the plays for it, and other people did also. And at Christmas time, when it snowed properly, which

it did, we had a pantomime into which was introduced a toy called Pharaoh's Serpents, little brown things like eggs which, when lit, uncoiled and produced curling, writhing snakes. And there were Japanese daylight fireworks. And though the figures were slid on to the stage on tin slides, and spoke without moving, still they held magic for me, and I have not lost, thank God, my sense of magic now.

from

Over the Gate

MISS READ

This second extract from the works of the Berkshire author Miss Read also takes us to the fictional village of Fairacre. The Second World War had been over for several years, and it had become the custom for Fairacre Women's Institute to hold an annual reunion in the village hall for the former evacuee families from London who had once been billeted in the village. On this occasion the reunion had just ended, and both visitors and villagers alike were happily replete with tea and cakes and a surfeit of gossip about their shared wartime experiences. It was all too obvious, however, that there was no love lost between two of the company, former evacuee Mrs Jarman, a spritely down-to-earth Cockney, and Fairacre's school caretaker, the formidable Mrs Pringle. They openly hated each other, as they

had done during the war, and it was a situation which puzzled
the village schoolmistress who had only come to Fairacre fairly
recently. She therefore sought an explanation from her friend
Mrs Willet, who recalled how the feud had come to a head
during a wartime jumble sale in 1943. Mrs Jarman had been
in charge of the clothes stall and, among the items for sale were
three shirts donated by Mrs Pringle, all without any trace of
buttons. Much to Mrs Jarman's disgust, Mrs Pringle defiantly
admitted that she had removed all the buttons to save them as a
gesture to help the war effort! Mrs Jarman reacted with bitter
Cockney sarcasm, and she was not to forget the incident. The
sequel was to come a few months after the jumble sale, and it
was all to do with Mrs Pringle's Christmas pudding . . .

Some months after the sale, the good ladies of Fairacre
Women's Institute decided to make their Christmas puddings
together. They worked out that the whole process would be
much cheaper if they made the mixture in one batch and
cooked all the puddings in the large electric copper.

The recipe, cut from a daily paper, made grisly reading to
those used to the normal ingredients of pre-war puddings. No
brandy, stout, fresh eggs or butter appeared in the 1943
recipe. Instead, such dreadful items as grated carrot,
margarine, dried egg powder and – the final touch of horror –
'a tablespoonful of gravy browning to enrich the colour',
figured on the depressing list of ingredients.

But times were hard, and years of privation had blunted the
sensibilities of even the most fastidious. With much
cheerfulness the ladies set about their preparations for making
'An Economical and Nutritious Wartime Christmas Pudding'.

Dozens of pudding basins, each bearing its owner's name on
adhesive tape stuck on the base, waited on the long tables. Little
paper bags bearing treasured ounces of currants and sultanas,
mixed spices, breadcrumbs and two precious fresh lemons,

jostled each other near the enormous yellow mixing bowl from the Vicarage. By ten o'clock the ingredients were being stirred zealously by half a dozen helpers, most of them elderly women, for the majority were doing war work of some sort or other. Mrs Willet busily greased the basins with carefully-hoarded margarine papers, listening to the chatter about her.

'We'll set the copper to *very slow*,' said the vicar's wife, 'and then it should be perfectly safe until tea time. Mrs Willet's staying until eleven-thirty, to make sure it's simmering properly and then the rota begins.'

It had been arranged that one or other of the W.I. members should look in every hour to see that all was well, and to top up the water in the copper if it was getting too low. Christmas puddings were too precious to be left entirely to themselves for such a length of time.

By eleven, the puddings were ready for immersion. Every household in Fairacre had one, and some had two or three, standing in the water. This was the Women's Institute's practical help towards Christmas, and very well planned the organisation had been.

'Here's Mrs Pringle's,' said Mrs Willet, bearing a stout two-pounder to the copper. She peered underneath the basin to read the big black capitals on the tape, before letting it down gently beside the others.

'Then that's the last,' said the vicar's wife thankfully. 'Just time to have a cup of tea before we knock off.'

It was very quiet when they had gone. Mrs Willet took out her knitting and sat by the humming copper. The clock said twenty past eleven and she had promised to stay until half past. As she knitted, she read the list of names pinned on the wall by the copper. During the afternoon she saw that Mrs Pringle and Mrs Jarman were due to call in. Both worked in the mornings and had been unable to stir their own puddings this year.

'2.30 – Mrs Pringle.'

'3.30 – Mrs Parr' (only that would be her maid, Mrs Willet surmised), and –

'4.30 – Mrs Jarman' who would no doubt rush back to her family in time to fry the inevitable chips on which that ebullient household seemed to exist.

'5.30 – anyone welcome.' This was when the puddings would be lifted out and handed to their lucky owners. Mrs Willet had promised to help with this chore.

At twenty-five to twelve she lifted the lid, noted with relief that the water was bubbling gently, checked all the switches, wrote a note to the next pudding-minder saying *'25 to 12. Everything all right. Alice Willet'*, and made her way back through the village.

At five-thirty a throng of women crowded the steamy hall collecting their basins and lodging them in shopping baskets, string bags or the baskets on the front of bicycles.

'Got the right one?' called Mrs Jarman to Mrs Pringle, as she watched that lady peering under the basins for her name. 'Bet you've got more fruit in yours than the rest of us!'

Mrs Pringle sniffed and ignored the quip. Depositing her pudding in the black depths of her oilcloth shopping bag, she passed majestically from the hall without deigning to reply.

The fantastic sequel to the pudding-making session might never have been known to Fairacre but for an unusually generous gesture of Mrs Pringle's.

As Christmas Day approached she heard that a large party of the Jarmans' friends were proposing to spend the day next door.

'My heart fair bleeds for poor Jane Morgan,' said Mrs Pringle lugubriously to her son John. 'She'll be crowded out of house and home, as far as I can see. I've a good mind to invite her round here for Christmas dinner.'

Neither Corporal Pringle nor Private Morgan were to be given Christmas leave. Mrs Pringle's sister and a schoolgirl

niece, much the same age as John, were coming from Caxley for the day, and as the sister and Jane Morgan knew each other well, it seemed a good idea to ask their neighbour to join the party. Jane Morgan was gratefully surprised, and accepted.

The pudding simmered all the morning, and most delightful aromas crept about the kitchen, for there was a duck roasting in the oven as well as the 'nutritious wartime' delicacy on top of the hob. Mrs Pringle and her sister had a good gossip, their children played amicably with their new presents, and except for the ear-splitting racket occasioned by the crowd next door, the benevolent spirit of Christmas hung over all. At twelve-thirty Jane Morgan appeared, thankful to be out of her noisy home, and they all sat down to dinner.

The duck was excellent. The pudding looked wonderful. Mrs Pringle plunged a knife into its gravy-darkened top and cut the first slice.

'Mum!' squeaked John excitedly. 'There's something shining!'

'Sh!' said his aunt. 'Don't give the game away! Perhaps it's a sixpence.'

'The pudding looked wonderful . . .'

Mrs Pringle looked puzzled.

'No sixpences in this pudding!' she said. 'In any case, I don't hold with metal objects in food. I always wraps up anything like that in a morsel of greaseproof.'

She put the first slice on a plate for Mrs Morgan. There was certainly a suspicious chinking sound as the pudding met the china surface.

'When I was little,' said Jane Morgan, 'we used to have dear little china dolls in our Christmas pudding. No bigger than an inch, they were! With shiny black heads. We used to put them in the dolls' house, I remember.'

But Jane Morgan's reminiscences were being ignored, for all eyes were on the pudding. There was no doubt about it, there were a great many shiny foreign objects among the other wartime ingredients. Mrs Pringle's breathing became more stertorous as the slices were cut. She sat down heavily in front of the last plate, her own, and then spoke.

'Just pick it over before you take a mouthful. I reckons someone's been playing tricks on us.'

Spoons and forks twitched the glutinous mass back and forth, amidst amazed cries from the assembled company. When they came to count up the foreign objects they found no fewer than two dozen mother of pearl shirt buttons.

Mrs Pringle said not a word, but opened a tin of pineapple chunks instead.

Late that night, when the Jarmans' company had roared away and the children had been chased to bed, Mrs Jarman met her landlady in the communal kitchen. Jane Morgan was in her husband's dressing gown, her wispy hair was in a small pigtail, and her teeth had been left upstairs in a glass of water. She was busy filling a hot water bottle.

'Had a good time?' asked Mrs Jarman boisterously. 'We have. Never laughed so much since I came here.'

'That's nice!' said Mrs Morgan politely. 'Yes, I enjoyed it

next door, but there was something wrong with the Christmas pudding.'

Mrs Jarman drew in her breath sharply.

'What was up with it?' she enquired.

'It was absolutely stuffed with shirt buttons,' said Mrs Morgan, wide-eyed. 'Mrs Pringle was dumbfounded.'

'Shirt buttons,' echoed Mrs Jarman. She broke into peals of noisy laughter.

'Ah well,' she gasped, through her spasms, 'that should please the old trout! She told me once that she saved shirt buttons!'

Still laughing, she made her way upstairs, followed by her mystified landlady.

Christmas Eve, 1916

E. SHARWOOD SMITH

The following verse, dated 'Newbury, 1916', is one of several written by E. Sharwood Smith during the years of the First World War and published later as part of an anthology of his work. Entitled 'Christmas Eve, 1916', it was dedicated to a recipient identified only as 'E.C.', and evokes all the peace of the Berkshire countryside at a time when so much of the world was being subjected to the horrors of war.

A Berkshire Christmas

I leaned on a gate,
And there to my view
Was a fairy picture
Nature drew,
And I thought I would paint it
And send it you.

The purple distance,
The laughing valleys,
With the new wine poured
From a golden chalice,
The ridgeway climbing
Through phantom mist,
All topaz, emerald,
Amethyst,
The red-roofed cottage,
The elm trees seven,
That waved their greetings
To God in heaven.

A far bell pealing,
The plaintive cry
Of a plover wheeling
Twixt earth and sky,
A lone rook homing,
The first faint stir
Of the new life coming
In earth and air.
And the spirit that sings
To all that list,
Whose hearts have partaken
Love's eucharist.

Cried 'Mourn no longer!
I hear a voice
The far low whisper,
That bids rejoice.'
And now I hear it,
Now lost once more,
The longed-for footfall
So loved of yore,
Of the dear glad angel
Bringing again
'Peace upon earth
Goodwill to men.'

from

The Golden Age

KENNETH GRAHAME

This second extract from the works of Kenneth Grahame comes from a book which, in many respects, is autobiographical, as it relates the story of parentless children living in a country house under the eagle eye of a strict governess. This was similar to the fate which befell the young Kenneth, his sister Helen and his brothers William and Roland, who were sent by their father to live with their maternal grandmother at Cookham Dean after their mother had died following a serious illness. In The

Golden Age, the names of the children are changed and the governess takes the place of the grandmother, but many other similarities to Kenneth Grahame's own childhood are retained. The chapter reproduced here relates the children's adventures at a time when a severe snowstorm had marooned them indoors shortly after the excitement of the twelve days of Christmas had come to an end. It provides a fascinating insight into how middle-class children amused themselves in the second half of the last century, long before the arrival of the television set and the electronic games which now dominate childhood entertainment.

Twelfth Night had come and gone, and life next morning seemed a trifle flat and purposeless. But yester-eve, and the mummers were here! They had come striding into the old kitchen, powdering the red-brick floor with snow from their barbaric bedizenments; and stamping, and crossing, and declaiming, till all was whirl and riot and shout.

Harold was frankly afraid: unabashed, he buried himself in cook's ample bosom. Edward feigned a manly superiority to illusion, and greeted these awful apparitions familiarly, as Dick and Harry and Joe. As for me, I was too big to run, too rapt to resist the magic and surprise.

Whence came these outlanders, breaking in on us with song and ordered masque and a terrible clashing of wooden swords? And after these, what strange visitants might we not look for any quiet night, when the chestnuts popped in the ashes, and the old ghost stories drew the awestricken circle close? Old Merlin, perhaps, 'all furred in black sheepskins, and a russet gown, with a bow and arrows, and bearing wild geese in his hand!' Or stately Ogier the Dane, recalled from Faery, asking his way to the land that once had need of him! Or even, on some white night, the Snow Queen herself, with a chime of sleigh-bells and the patter of reindeer's feet,

halting of a sudden at the door flung wide, while aloft the Northern Lights went shaking attendant spears among the quiet stars!

This morning, housebound by the relentless and indefatigable snow, I was feeling the reaction. Edward, on the contrary, being violently stage-struck on this his first introduction to the real Drama, was striding up and down the floor, proclaiming 'Here be I, King George the Third', in a strong Berkshire accent. Harold, accustomed, as the youngest, to lonely antics and to sports that asked no sympathy, was absorbed in 'clubmen': a performance consisting in a measured progress round the room arm-in-arm with an imaginary companion of reverend years, with

The result of a Christmas Day blizzard in 1927 near the Thames-side village of Pangbourne. This was an area of Berkshire that was well known to Kenneth Grahame and from which he gained much of his inspiration as a writer

occasional halts at imaginary clubs, where – imaginary steps being leisurely ascended – imaginary papers were glanced at, imaginary scandal was discussed with elderly shakings of the head, and – regrettable to say – imaginary glasses were lifted lipwards.

Heaven only knows how the germ of this weary pastime first found way into his small-boyish being. It was his own invention, and he was proportionately proud of it.

Meanwhile, Charlotte and I, crouched in the window-seat, watched, spell-stricken, the whirl and eddy and drive of the innumerable snowflakes, wrapping our cheery little world in an uncanny uniform, ghastly in line and hue.

Charlotte was sadly out of spirits. Having 'countered' Miss Smedley at breakfast, during some argument or other, by an apt quotation from her favourite classic (*The Fairy Book*), she had been gently but firmly informed that no such things as fairies ever really existed.

'Do you mean to say it's all lies?' asked Charlotte bluntly. Miss Smedley deprecated the use of any such unladylike words in any connecion at all.

'These stories had their origin, my dear,' she explained, 'in a mistaken anthropomorphism in the interpretation of nature. But though we are now too well informed to fall into similar errors, there are still many beautiful lessons to be learned from these myths . . .'

'But how can you learn anything,' persisted Charlotte, 'from what doesn't exist?' And she left the table defiant, howbeit depressed.

'Don't you mind *her*,' I said consolingly; 'how can she know anything about it? Why, she can't even throw a stone properly!'

'Edward says they're all rot, too,' replied Charlotte doubtfully.

'Edward says everything's rot,' I explained, 'now he thinks

he's going into the army. If a thing's in a book it *must* be true, so that settles it!'

Charlotte looked almost reassured. The room was quieter now, for Edward had got the dragon down and was boring holes in him with a purring sound; Harold was ascending the steps of the Athenaeum with a jaunty air – suggestive rather of the Junior Carlton. Outside, the tall elm-tops were hardly to be seen through the feathery storm.

'The sky's a-falling,' quoted Charlotte softly; 'I must go and tell the king.' The quotation suggested a fairy story, and I offered to read to her, reaching out for the book. But the Wee Folk were under a cloud; sceptical hints had embittered the chalice. So I was fain to fetch *Arthur* – second favourite with Charlotte for his dames riding errant, and an easy first with us boys for his spear-splintering crash of tourney and hurtle against hopeless odds.

Here again, however, I proved unfortunate; what ill-luck made the book open at the sorrowful history of Balin and Balan? 'And he vanished anon,' I read: 'and so he heard an horne blow, as it had been the death of a beast. "That blast," said Balin, "is blowen for me, for I am the prize, and yet am I not dead."'

Charlotte began to cry: she knew the rest too well. I shut the book in despair. Harold emerged from behind the armchair. He was sucking his thumb (a thing which members of the Reform are seldom seen to do), and he stared wide-eyed at his tear-stained sister. Edward put off his histrionics, and rushed up to her as the consoler – a new part for him.

'I know a jolly story,' he began. 'Aunt Eliza told it me. It was when she was somewhere over in that beastly abroad' (he had once spent a black month of misery at Dinan) 'and there was a fellow there who had got two storks. And one stork died – it was the she-stork.' ('What did it die of?' put in Harold.) 'And the other stork was quite sorry, and moped, and went on, and got very miserable. So they looked about and found a

duck, and introduced it to the stork. The duck was a drake, but the stork didn't mind, and they loved each other and were as jolly as could be. By and by another duck came along – a real she-duck this time – and when the drake saw her he fell in love, and left the stork and went and proposed to the duck, for she was very beautiful. But the poor stork who was left, he said nothing at all to anybody, but just pined and pined and pined away, till one morning he was found quite dead. But the ducks lived happily ever afterwards!'

This was Edward's idea of a jolly story! Down again went the corners of poor Charlotte's mouth. Really, Edward's stupid inability to see the real point in anything was *too* annoying! It

'The indefatigable snow . . .' – Victorian Caversham on the banks of Kenneth Grahame's beloved Thames, a few days after Christmas in 1887

was always so. Years before, it being necessary to prepare his youthful mind for a domestic event that might lead to awkward questionings at a time when there was little leisure to invent appropriate answers, it was delicately inquired of him whether he would like to have a little brother, or perhaps a little sister?

He considered the matter carefully in all its bearings, and finally declared for a Newfoundland pup. Any boy more 'gleg at the uptak' would have met his parents halfway, and eased their burden. As it was, the matter had to be approached all over again from a fresh standpoint. And now, while Charlotte turned away sniffingly, with a hiccup that told of an overwrought soul, Edward, unconscious of the mischief he had done, wheeled round on Harold with a shout.

'I want a live dragon,' he announced. 'You've got to be my dragon!'

'Leave me go, will you?' squealed Harold, struggling stoutly. 'I'm playin' at something else. How can I be a dragon and belong to all the clubs?'

'But wouldn't you like to be a nice scaly dragon, all green,' said Edward, trying persuasion, 'with a curly tail and red eyes, and breathing real smoke and fire?'

Harold wavered an instant: Pall Mall was still strong in him. The next he was grovelling on the floor. No saurian ever swung a tail so scaly and so curly as his. Clubland was a thousand years away. With horrific pants he emitted smokiest smoke and fiercest fire.

'Now I want a princess,' cried Edward, clutching Charlotte ecstatically; 'and *you* can be the doctor, and heal me from the dragon's deadly wound.'

Of all professions, I held the sacred art of healing in worst horror and contempt. Cataclysmal memories of purge and draught crowded thick on me, and with Charlotte – who courted no barren honours – I made a break for the door.

Edward did likewise, and the hostile forces clashed together on the mat, and for a brief space things were mixed and chaotic and Arthurian.

The silvery sound of the luncheon bell restored an instant peace, even in the teeth of clenched antagonisms like ours. The Holy Grail itself, 'sliding athwart a sunbeam', never so effectually stilled a riot of warring passions into sweet and quiet accord.

Christmas Entertaining

ANNE FOX

In our modern age of supermarkets, freezers, microwaves and so-called convenience foods, the seasonal ritual of preparing festive fare may be a good deal simpler than it once was, but it has surely lost much of the excitement and anticipation which were all part of the magic of Christmas before 'progress' changed the character of the kitchen for ever. Back in the 1930s, for instance (as journalist Anne Fox discovered when she delved into the subject), the variety of imaginative culinary delights for Christmas being offered to readers of The Reading Review *would nowadays test the ingenuity – and the patience – of even the most dedicated cook.*

Each Christmas, the magazine dutifully plied its readers with a tempting array of seasonal recipes, contributed by an expert named Nora J. Bastin. So that readers were left in no doubt that she was *bona fide* and knew a thing or two about the finer points of the culinary art, her credentials were printed alongside her name: Diplomée Domestic Science.

She called her column 'Christmas Entertaining', and in the edition for December 1938 she was evidently determined to ensure that her readers and their guests would be more than agreeably sated by the time the festive season was over.

'It is in keeping with the kindly spirit of the time,' she enthused, 'that we should keep open house at Christmas, and that every guest should be welcomed warmly and plied with the best food and drink we can offer.'

She described her first suggestion as 'something new for breakfast' in the shape of fish brawn. This was presumably for the benefit of those who were expecting their guests to stay on for a day or so, rather than for any casual callers who happened to knock on the door as early as breakfast time. The latter would no doubt have found their seasonal *joie de vivre* under some strain, had they been greeted with 'Merry Christmas! Come in. Have some fish brawn.'

'Flake ¾ lb of white fish,' wrote the resourceful Nora Bastin, 'removing any bone or skin, then slice thinly two hard-boiled eggs. Wet a plain mould or basin and coat thinly with well-flavoured aspic jelly. Fill with alternate layers of seasoned fish, mixed with a little lemon juice and grated nutmeg, and sliced seasoned eggs, finishing with a layer of fish. Strain over enough aspic jelly to fill the mould, and leave to set. Turn out and garnish with sprigs of parsley and quartered tomatoes.'

The next suggestion was for a veal galantine, certainly a little more versatile than fish brawn, as it was described as 'a good stand-by for it can appear at breakfast, lunch or supper, and serve as sandwich filling on odd occasions besides'.

The list of ingredients included a small breast of veal, 2 lbs of sausages, ½ lb cooked ham, 3 hard-boiled eggs, salt, pepper, nutmeg, a few pistachios or almonds, and a little grated lemon rind.

'Bone the veal, then add nutmeg and lemon rind to the sausage meat after removing the skins. Spread the sausage meat on the veal, adding the ham cut in strips and the eggs cut in quarters. Fill up the spaces with almonds or pistachios, season well and roll up and tie in place with string. Tie in a buttered cloth and simmer in stock for about 2½ to 3 hours. Then remove the cloth, tie in a clean cloth and press between weighted boards until cold. Trim and remove string. Coat with a chaudfroid sauce, then with aspic jelly, and garnish as desired.'

What to do with the remains of the turkey after Christmas Day seems to have been no less of a problem in 1938 than it is today, and Nora Bastin came to the rescue with a recipe for turkey croquettes.

'Allow 3 ozs of cooked ham or tongue to 6 ozs of cold cooked turkey. Mince both finely and season well. Add 3 teaspoonsful of chopped parsley, 1 teaspoonful of chopped onion, and a little grated nutmeg. Moisten with good brown gravy or tomato sauce, and add a beaten egg. Heat gently in a small pan, taking care not to curdle the egg. Spread the mixture on a floured plate, mark in twelve portions and leave till cold. Shape each portion into a small roll or ball, and coat with egg and breadcrumbs twice. Fry in deep fat until nicely browned, drain well and serve very hot, garnished with fried parsley and small bacon rolls, fried mushrooms or tomatoes.'

For those who just couldn't cope with all that cooking so soon after Christmas Day, Nora came up with a cold alternative for using up the turkey. She called it winter salad.

'Remove the meat from the bone and cut into neat pieces. Mix with shredded celery and cubes of sweet apple. Season

The Christmas turkey, epitome of the traditional festive feast

and mix with mayonnaise sauce or salad cream. Pile on a bed of lettuce and garnish with bunches of cress and strips of sweet red pepper, or alternatively serve the mayonnaise mixture in hollowed tomato or apple cups.'

After this surfeit of savoury ideas, Nora Bastin evidently felt it was time to switch her attention to the sweeter side of festive fare, making the somewhat incontrovertible statement that 'creams, ices and jellies are popular Christmas sweets in addition to the traditional Christmas pudding, or as an

alternative sweet for those with whom such a rich pudding does not agree.'

Chestnuts, she maintained, are the basis of many delicious sweets, 'one of the nicest being coupes marrons, made with marrons glacés'. Readers were first instructed to soak a dozen marrons in a glass of sherry or their favourite liqueur. 'Break them with a fork and place a little in the bottom of six glasses. Add a spoonful of vanilla ice-cream or rich custard, pour over whipped cream flavoured with sherry or liqueur, and place a single marron on top for decoration.'

It sounds arguable that this rich concoction was, in fact, any easier to digest than Christmas pudding, although Nora's next dessert suggestion, coffee and ginger cream, was certainly a little less exotic. This, she wrote, was 'excellent made with a pint packet of lemon, orange or vanilla jelly, 1 pint of milk, 2 tablespoonsful of coffee essence and 2 ozs of glacé ginger. Make the jelly with hot, not boiling, milk, taking care not to curdle it. Leave in a cool place until thick, but not yet set, then add the ginger cut into small pieces. Pour into a wetted mould or individual glasses, and leave till set. Serve with thick cream flavoured with essence of ginger.'

To end her seasonal contribution that year, Nora Bastin concentrated on cakes, predicting that a variety of them 'will be in demand at the Christmas tea table'. 'The Christmas cake itself,' she added, 'is usually so rich that it can only be indulged in with moderation, so that old-fashioned cakes, such as seed, Madeira and cherry, make an excellent foil to its richness.' Quite so.

Her first antidote for rich Christmas cake was called Christmas baskets. 'Bake a good sponge or Genoese mixture in a flat tin,' she explained, 'and when cold, cut in rounds about 2 inches in diameter. Have ready about 6 ozs almond paste which should be rolled out on a board dusted with icing sugar until very thin. Cut two rounds for each cake, slightly

larger than the tops, and a strip of paste of the same depth as the cakes, and long enough to wrap round the sides, allowing for a neat join. Brush the sides of the cakes with warm jam and press the strips of paste on each. Deal with the top and bottom of each little cake in the same way, so that the whole of each cake is enclosed in almond paste. Take a fork and press the prongs into the paste to represent basket-weaving round the sides and top. Very little skill is required to achieve a good effect. Then decorate each basket with a spray of holly or mistletoe made with coloured almond paste.'

Nora Bastin finally brought her column to a close with a fine flourish of Christmas cheer by revealing the recipe for cracker cake. It was made, she said, by covering a Swiss roll with coloured almond paste and was apparently 'a pleasing addition' to any children's party.

'For a medium-sized Swiss roll allow 6 to 8 ozs of paste. Roll it thinly as before, in an oblong shape, large enough to wrap round the cake and project 3 inches at each end. With a sharp knife make a fringe at each end while the paste is flat on the board. Then brush the cake with jam and roll it in the paste so that the join is at the bottom and the fringed ends project beyond the cake. Pinch these ends with the fingers to resemble the ends of a cracker, and tie with coloured ribbon, real or made with almond paste. The effect,' confirmed Nora Bastin,'is decidedly unusual, but not at all difficult to achieve.'

One cannot help wondering how this good lady, with her impressive Diplomée Domestic Science, would react today if she could visit one of our modern supermarkets a few days before Christmas. She would probably be quite impressed, if not a little bemused, by the sheer galaxy of exotic seasonal goodies, temptingly packaged and invitingly displayed in their colourful seasonal finery. But would she really appreciate them? I somehow doubt it. For her, I suspect, the ritual and

excitement of creating traditional festive fare in her own kitchen would still be an essential element of any Christmas celebrations worth their name.

Perhaps those of us who regularly complain that Christmas isn't what it used to be, could do worse than gain just a little inspiration from Nora J. Bastin. Although maybe we should draw the line at offering our Christmas guests fish brawn for breakfast.

A Christmas Party

MARY RUSSELL MITFORD

In this second extract from Our Village, *Mary Russell Mitford's delightful chronicle of country life in the early nineteenth century, we witness the preparations for a Christmas party being planned by an itinerant fishmonger, Jacob Frost, partly to celebrate his recent marriage to Hester Hewit. Hester is the landlady at one of the village's 'respectable hostelries', The Bell, an establishment which Jacob, with his extravagant tastes, sees as an ideal location for some no-expense-spared seasonal junketings. Hester, on the other hand, accustomed to a more frugal lifestyle, is somewhat less enthusiastic. In relating how the situation resolves itself, Mary Russell Mitford's keen perception of human behaviour is given full rein. We join the story a few days after the wedding, as Jacob, accompanied by Hester, makes his way through the village to The Bell.*

Before he reached The Bell he had formed, and communicated to Hester, the spirited resolution of giving a splendid party in the Christmas week — a sort of wedding feast or house-warming, consisting of smoking and cards for the old, dancing and singing for the young, and eating and drinking for all ages. In spite of Hester's decided disapprobation, invitations were given and preparations entered on forthwith.

Sooth to say, such are the sad contradictions of poor human nature, that Mrs Frost's displeasure, albeit a bride in the honeymoon, not only entirely failed in persuading Master Frost to change his plan, but even seemed to render him more confirmed and resolute in his purpose.

Hester was a thrifty housewife, and although Jacob was apparently, after his fashion, a very gallant and affectionate husband, and although her interest had now become his — and of his own interest none had ever suspected him to be careless — yet he did certainly take a certain sly pleasure in making an attack at once on her hoards and her habits, and forcing her into a gaiety and an outlay which made the poor bride start back aghast.

The full extent of Hester's misfortune in this ball did not, however, come upon her at once. She had been accustomed to the speculating hospitality of the Christmas parties at The Rose, whose host was wont at tide times to give a supper to his customers, that is to say, to furnish the eatables thereof — the leg of mutton and turnips, the fat goose and apple sauce, and the huge plum puddings, of which light viands that meal usually consisted — on an understsanding that the aforesaid customers were to pay for the drinkables therewith consumed. From the length of the sittings, as well as the reports current on such occasions, Hester was pretty well assured that the expenditure had been most judicious, and that the leg of mutton and trimmings had been paid for over and over.

She herself being, as she expressed it, 'a lone woman, and apt to be put upon', had never gone further in these matters than a cup of hyson and muffins, and a glass of hot elder-wine, to some of her cronies in the neighbourhood. But having considerable confidence both in the extent of Jacob's connections and their tippling propensities, as well as in that faculty of getting tipsy and making tipsy in Jacob himself, which she regarded 'with one auspicious and one dropping eye', as good and bad for her trade, she had at first no very great objection to try for once the experiment of a Christmas party; nor was she so much startled at the idea of a dance – dancing, as she observed, being a mighty provoker of thirst; neither did she very greatly object to her husband's engaging old Timothy, the fiddler, to officiate for the evening, on condition of giving him as much ale as he chose to drink, although she perfectly well knew what that promise implied; Timothy's example being valuable on such an occasion.

But when the dreaded truth stared her in the face, that this entertainment was to be a bona fide treat – that not only the leg of mutton, the fat goose, and the plum puddings, but the ale, wine, spirits and tobacco were to come out of her coffers, then party, dancing, and fiddler became nuisances past endurance, the latter above all.

Old Timothy was a person of some note in our parish, known to every man, woman and child in the place, of which, indeed, he was a native. He had been a soldier in his youth, and having had the good luck to receive a sabre wound on his skull, had been discharged from the service as infirm of mind, and passed to his parish accordingly. Here he led a wandering, pleasant sort of life, sometimes in one public house, sometimes in another – tolerated, as Hester said, for his bad example, until he had run up a score that became intolerable, at which times he was turned out, with the workhouse to go to, for a *pis aller*, and a comfortable prospect that his good

humour, his good fellowship and his fiddle would in process of time be missed and wanted, and that he might return to his old haunts and run up a fresh score.

When half tipsy, which happened nearly every day in the week, and at all hours, he would ramble up and down the village, playing snatches of tunes at every corner, and collecting about him a never-failing audience of urchins of either sex, amongst which small mob old Timothy, with his jokes, his songs and his antics, was incredibly popular.

Against justice and constable, treadmill and stocks, the sabre cut was a protection, although I must candidly confess that I do not think the crack in the crown ever made itself visible in his demeanour until a sufficient quantity of ale had gone down his throat to account for any aberration of conduct.

In short, old Timothy was a privileged person; and terrible sot though he were, he almost deserved to be so, for his good humour, his contentedness, his constant festivity of temper, and his goodwill towards every living thing – a goodwill which met with its usual reward in being heartily and universally returned.

Everybody liked old Timothy, with the solitary exception of the hostess of The Bell, who, having once had him as an inmate during three weeks, had been so scandalized by his disorderly habits, that, after having with some difficulty turned him out of her house, she had never admitted him into it again. She had actually resorted to the expedient of buying off her intended customer, even when he presented himself pence in hand, by the gift of a pint of home-brewed at the door, rather than suffer him to effect a lodgement in her tap-room – a mode of dismissal so much to Timothy's taste that his incursions had become more and more frequent, insomuch that 'to get rid of the fiddler and other scapegraces who were apt to put upon a lone woman', formed a main article in the catalogue of reasons assigned by Hester to herself and the world, for her marriage with Jacob Frost.

Accordingly, the moment she heard that Timothy's irregularities and ill example were likely to prove altogether unprofitable, she revived her old objection to the poor fiddler's morals, rescinded her consent to his admission, and insisted so vehemently on his being unordered, that her astonished husband, fairly out-talked and out-scolded, was fain to purchase a quiet evening by a promise of obedience.

Hester's apparent success in barring Timothy from the list of guests gave her renewed confidence to ban another villager from the celebrations. This was the widow Martha Glen, proprietor of the village bakery and chandler's shop. Hester and Martha had long been sworn enemies, a situation fostered as much by malicious and largely unfounded village gossip as by any specific facts. Hester was adamant, however. The widow Glen was not to be invited.

On Hester's conditioning that Mrs Glen should be excluded from the party, Jacob just gave himself a wink and a nod, twisted his mouth a little more on one side than usual, and assented without a word; and with the same facility did he relinquish the bough of mistletoe, which he had purposed to suspend from the bacon rack – the ancient mistletoe bough, on passing under which our village lads are apt to snatch a kiss from the village maidens: a ceremony which offended Hester's nicety, and which Jacob promised to abrogate.

Pacified by these concessions, the bride promised to make due preparation for the ball, whilst the bridegroom departed on his usual expedition to the coast.

Of the unrest of that week of bustling preparation, words can give but a faint image. Oh, the scourings, the cleanings, the sandings, the dustings, the scoldings of that disastrous week! The lame ostler and the red-haired parish girl were worked off their feet – 'even Sunday shone no Sabbath day to

them', for then did the lame ostler trudge eight miles to the church of a neighbouring parish, to procure the attendance of a celebrated bassoon player to officiate in lieu of Timothy; whilst the poor little maid was sent nearly as far to the next town, in quest of an itinerant show-woman, of whom report had spoken at The Bell, to beat the tambourine.

The show-woman proved undiscoverable, but the bassoon player, having promised to come, and to bring with him a clarinet, Mrs Frost was at ease as to her music; and having provided more victuals than the whole village could have discussed at a sitting, and having moreover adorned her house with berried holly, china roses and chrysanthemums after the most tasteful manner, began to enter into the spirit of the thing, and to wish for the return of her husband, to admire and to praise.

Late on the great day Jacob arrived, his cart laden with marine stores, for his share of the festival. Never had our goodly village witnessed such a display of oysters, mussels, periwinkles and cockles, to say nothing of apples and nuts, and two little kegs, snugly covered up, which looked exceedingly as if they had cheated the revenue, a packet of green tea, which had something of the same air, and a new silk gown, of a flaming salmon colour, straight from Paris, which he insisted on Hester's retiring to assume, whilst he remained to arrange the table and receive the company, who, it being now about four o'clock p.m. – our good rustics can never have enough of a good thing – were beginning to assemble for the ball.

The afternoon was fair and cold, and dry and frosty, and the Matthewses, Bridgwaters, Whites and Joneses, in short the whole farmerage and shopkeepery of the place, with a goodly proportion of wives and daughters, came pouring in apace.

Jacob received them with much gallantry, uncloaking and unbonneting the ladies, assisted by his two staring and

awkward auxiliaries, welcoming their husbands and fathers, and apologizing, as best he might, for the absence of his helpmate; who, 'perplexed in the extreme' by her new finery which, happening to button down the back, she was fain to put on hind side before, did not make her appearance till the greater part of the company had arrived, and the music had struck up a country dance.

An evil moment, alas! did poor Hester choose for her entry: for the first sound that met her ear was Timothy's fiddle, forming a strange trio with the bassoon and the clarinet; and the first persons whom she saw were Tom Higgs cracking walnuts at the chimney-side, and Sandy Frazer saluting the widow Glen under the mistletoe.

How she survived such sights and sounds does appear wonderful – but survive them she did, for at three o'clock a.m., she was engaged in a sociable game at cards, which, by the description, seems to have been long whist, with the identical widow Glen, Sandy Frazer and William Ford, and had actually won fivepence halfpenny of Martha's money.

The young folks were still dancing gaily, to the sound of Timothy's fiddle, which fiddle had the good quality of going on almost as well drunk as sober, and it was now playing solo, the clarinet being *hors de combat* and the bassoon under the table.

Tom Higgs, after showing off more tricks than a monkey, amongst the rest sewing the whole card party together by the skirts, to the probable damage of Mrs Frost's gay gown, had returned to his old post by the fire, and his old amusement of cracking walnuts, with the shells of which he was pelting the little parish girl, who sat fast asleep on the other side.

Jacob Frost, in all his glory, sat in a cloud of tobacco smoke, roaring out catches with his old friend George Bridgwater and half a dozen other cronies, whilst 'aye the ale was growing better', and the Christmas party went merrily on.

Santa Steams In

COLIN COX

*The important railway junction of Didcot, historically
in Berkshire although now transferred by boundary
changes into Oxfordshire, has never forgotten its
traditional links with the old Great Western Railway.
These continue through the activities of the Great
Western Society which attracts railway enthusiasts and
their families from all over the country to its popular
Didcot Railway Centre. The welcome they receive is never
warmer than at Christmastime, and this is the setting
for the following delightful seasonal story related by
children's author Colin Cox.*

It was back in the 1970s that Santa Claus first discovered the
Didcot Railway Centre. He had been on a reconnoitring trip
to Berkshire and the surrounding counties in preparation for
his main visit on Christmas Eve, which was still a few days
away. The weather was cold and blustery, and it had started to
snow heavily, conditions that both he and his faithful team of
reindeer were normally quite used to, for that's what it was
like most of the time back home.

But heavy snow did have one problem. The poor visibility
made it all too easy to become disorientated.

On this particular night the situation was worsening by the
minute. Santa Claus was tired, and so were his reindeer as
they gamely pulled his sleigh through the low scudding
clouds. They were still a very long way from home.

There was nothing for it. They would just have to land somewhere for a rest. Better that than attempt to continue and possibly incur all the risks of a forced landing in some inhospitable place later on.

Santa Claus coaxed the reindeer a little lower as he peered through the driving snow, seeking somewhere to put the sleigh down safely. It was now well after midnight, and apart from a few dim street lamps casting arcs of lights on the white ground beneath them, there was little sign of life anywhere.

Time was running out. He was now so low that he could pick out individual buildings and other features on the ground, and in any case the exhausted reindeer could scarcely summon up enough energy to carry on much further.

It was then that Santa Claus noticed a likely landing place almost directly below. It seemed to be surrounded by what looked like the parallel ridges of snow-covered railway lines, but at least it was just large enough to put the sleigh down safely. With a deft flick of the reins, he skilfully guided the reindeer round in a tight circle and glided to the ground with hardly a bump.

For a moment or so he sat there regaining his breath, while the grateful reindeer panted noisily as they rested their weary limbs.

Santa Claus knew he could not afford to stay here long. If someone were to discover him, with Christmas still some way off, it would be embarrassing to say the least. But it was unlikely, he thought, that anyone would be around so late on a night like this.

What he needed most, apart from a rest, was some water for his thirsty reindeer, so he decided to have a quick look round and try to discover where he was.

Despite the driving snow and the darkness, he very quickly realised he had landed in what he took to be some

sort of railway siding. Following one of the railway tracks for a few yards, he came across the snow-covered platform of what looked like a small country station. Not far away was a signal box, with a short flight of steps, each one bearing a deepening white carpet, leading up to its entrance.

But as he continued his exploration, it was his next discovery which intrigued Santa Claus most. There, rising above him in the driving snow was the massive bulk of a steam locomotive, reminiscent of those he remembered seeing on so many occasions in years gone by, during his Christmas excursions up and down the country.

Peeping into buildings nearby, he could just make out the unmistakable outline of similar great engines, and there were old railway carriages too.

Even in the darkness of a cold winter night, Santa Claus was enjoying himself. He was tempted to explore even further, but realised that time was passing all too quickly, and he still had a long journey in front of him. So, a little reluctantly, he started to make his way back to the waiting reindeer, still wondering exactly where he was, and marvelling at the unlikely surroundings in which he found himself.

It was then that he came across what looked like a large notice board, and as he screwed up his eyes against the snow, he could just make out that it bore three words: DIDCOT RAILWAY CENTRE.

So that's where I am, he said to himself, and then and there he vowed to come back as often as he could, as it was clearly the sort of place in which he could enjoy himself immensely.

It was as he was groping his way back through the darkness in the direction of the patiently waiting reindeer, that he almost walked straight into what he at first thought was an outsize lamp post. On further investigation, he discovered it

Santa Claus contributes to the
Christmas spirit at the Didcot
Railway Centre

was part of the once familiar apparatus used for filling the
water tanks of steam engines.

If this will replenish thirsty locomotives, he conjectured,
surely it will do the same for reindeer, and he plodded off to
fetch an old bucket he remembered having seen in the shelter
of a wall not far away. Then, one bucket at a time, he carried
the water to the waiting animals and allowed them to drink
their fill.

At last, refreshed and rested, they were ready to resume
their journey home, and as Santa Claus climbed on to the
sleigh he was pleased to note that it had now almost stopped
snowing.

Then, with a last look round and a quick crack of the whip,
he urged the reindeer up into the night sky and they were
away, heading for the north and home.

Santa Claus was as good as his word, and ever since that
fateful visit he has regularly returned to Didcot each

December, setting up his grotto actually on board a steam train, and dispensing his presents and seasonal cheer during the weekends running up to Christmas.

In fact, his visits have become one of the most popular of all the many events held at the Didcot Railway Centre, and the site is specially decorated for the occasion. To help him, Santa Claus has his special team of clowns, and he makes sure that every child who visits him receives a present as well as a soft drink and a chocolate, while the grown-ups have mulled cider and a mince pie.

There's plenty of carol singing too, with the help of local choirs, and the chance to enjoy unlimited train rides behind a real steam engine.

No-one enjoys these festive occasions more than Santa Claus himself, but he has never breathed a word to anyone about how he first discovered the Didcot Railway Centre on that snowy night all those years ago. That remains one of his best-kept secrets.

The people who run the Centre – the members of the Great Western Society – never did find out who had been responsible for those nocturnal footprints in the snow, or how that old bucket came to be left in the middle of the site, surrounded by the hoof-prints of some very strange animals indeed.

from

Tales of Old Berkshire

CECILIA MILLSON

Among the collection of delightful stories gathered together by Cecilia Millson for her anthology published in 1977, was the following account of a seventeenth-century Christmastide episode at Twyford, which is said to have resulted in the founding of a charity still in existence to this day.

The name of Edward Polehampton has been a household word in Twyford for over 250 years; ever since the foundations of three red-brick buildings were laid opposite the Rose and Crown Inn. How local interest must have been caught as the buildings grew into a school, chapel and master's house, and it was learned that it was a charitable foundation to benefit poor boys of the village.

Why did Mr Polehampton choose Twyford as the place for this generous gift? He never lived there, and appears to have had no connection at all with this village, once situated on the main Bath road to London, until a bypass released it from the continuous roar of traffic. To this day the riddle has never been clearly solved, but two tales are told, each giving a reason for his munificence.

One story relates that he was passing along the road to London with his young wife when she became ill. The landlord of the inn was kind to the invalid and her worried husband, and in gratitude for his hospitality, the village was remembered by Edward Polehampton when he was disposing of his wealth.

The second story, which is the most favoured, certainly provides good reason for the benefactor's concern for poor boys. It tells that he came to the village as a little lad, destitute and alone, and sank in despair on the doorstep of the Rose and Crown Inn. It was Christmas Eve in the year 1666. The landlord went to the door and found the pathetic child.

A 1920s snow scene at Twyford, the Berkshire village which still benefits from the charity set up by Edward Polehampton in the early eighteenth century

Was his heart stirred by thoughts of another child who found shelter at an inn, as he lifted the boy into the warmth of the room that Christmastide?

The kindly landlord cared for Edward Polehampton, fed and clothed him, until at last the lad was able to set out on the road to London. He went to seek his fortune, as so many boys have done throughout the centuries, but where many failed, Edward Polehampton succeeded.

Having become a pupil of a London painter, Henry Lyne, he was admitted to the Painter Stainers' Company and remained an honoured member until his death.

Unfortunately, little of Edward Polehampton's work remains. Although he painted some portraits, his work was chiefly centred on panels of allegorical and heraldic design. Very often these were used on the magnificent coaches of that period. He took pupils of his own, and was also a print-seller. He prospered and was able to buy property, thus adding to his wealth.

Edward Polehampton of the Parish of St Sepulchre, London, Citizen and Painter Stainer, made his will on the 27th day of July, 1721, by which time his charitable buildings at Twyford were already in the course of erection, and he made provision for them to be completed if he should die before that time.

The school was to house ten poor boys between the ages of eight and fifteen. Although a boy might leave before the age of fifteen if it was thought desirable, no pupil could remain after that age as the place had to be filled by a new boy. Every boy was to receive ten pounds a year for his clothing.

A master was to be appointed at a salary of forty pounds per annum, preferably a suitable minister of the Church of England who could also officiate at the chapel, where divine service was to be held every Sunday morning and afternoon. A sermon was to be preached at both services, which were to be attended by the boys of the school.

The benefactor realised that the minister might not wish to act as schoolmaster, in which case ten pounds were to be deducted from his salary and paid to another suitable man, who was then to live in the schoolmaster's house. In either case, boarders could be taken into the house in addition to the charity scholars, to supplement the master's income.

Four trustees were appointed – the Vicar of St Sepulchre, London; the Vicar of St Nicholas, Hurst; and the Vicar of St Mary's, Reading. These three trustees were for ever; the fourth, Dr William Skelton of Doctor's Commons, London, was appointed for his natural life.

No mention of a wife was made in the will, although it would seem that Edward Polehampton was reunited with some members of his family during his lifetime, for money was left to his nieces, Elizabeth Feelot and Mary Humphreys. Another woman, a Mrs Shore, also received a small legacy; it seems possible that she was his housekeeper. The executors, John Ford of London, Citizen and Bricklayer; Roger Askew of London, Citizen and Painter Stainer; and William Skelton of Doctor's Commons, received gifts for their trouble.

Edward Polehampton died in 1722 and in accordance with his wishes, was buried in the churchyard at St Nicholas's Church, Hurst. There was no church at Twyford at this time, and the school chapel must have been a blessing for those who wished to attend a service but found the long walk to Hurst too exhausting. Although the chapel was never consecrated, it was in use until the present church was built in Twyford in 1846.

A new state school was built in 1888, but it bears the name Polehampton School. Part of the charity school building remains to this day, opposite the private house which was once the Rose and Crown Inn. Did the donor choose the site of his school so that it was in the shadow of the hostelry? The charity still exists and is administered for the benefit of local children.

Perhaps one day the true answer will be found, and the reason for Polehampton's charity will be known for certain, but it will be difficult to replace the story of the landlord's Christmastide kindness which brought such benefit to the boys of Twyford.

Twyford's present-day Polehampton Infants' School can trace its origins back to the school built in 1888 to replace the original charity school. In the 1960s, a second school was built in the village – Polehampton County Junior – which also perpetuates the benefactor's name. The surviving part of the old charity school, mentioned by Cecilia Millson, is in fact the master's house, now converted, like the former Rose and Crown Inn, to private residential use.

Christmas Thoughts

WILLIAM WHITE

The old Reading Mercury *now belongs to newspaper history, but in its day it earned itself a loyal readership, not only for its coverage of the county's news, but for the regular non-news features which enlivened its pages. Among these was a longstanding series entitled 'Notes and Queries', edited by the*

*historian Ernest W. Dormer, which discussed a wide variety of
topics of county interest, often stimulated by letters from readers.
Each festive season the subjects inevitably focused on aspects of the
celebration of Christmas, and it was from among these that local
history writer William White gleaned the following extracts
when he delved into the archives. The first comes from 1957.*

OLD CHRISTMAS JUNKETINGS

If tradition does not lie, the quantities of food consumed in
the past centuries at Christmas by those who had the power
and the means to obtain it, must have been prodigious; and
this, in part, may account for the fact that, even in the days of
the Tudors, men were regarded as old at forty. The average
expectation of life was in a very much lower bracket than it is
today.

Scattered through ancient records we get glimpses of these
gargantuan repasts, and although it is not possible to be sure
of the number of retainers and guests taking part, a rough
calculation can sometimes be made, and this leaves little
doubt of the quantity of food consumed.

Here is an account of such a seasonal junketing. On Saturday,
31 December, 1289, Richard de Swinfield, Bishop of Hereford,
entered with his train through the noble gateway of Reading
Abbey. The Abbey was burdened with debt, but it is recorded
that the Abbot, Robert de Burghate, lived in great state and kept
his own domestic harper, named Hugh. The Bishop rewarded
Hugh with a present for his playing. The sound of the harp in
those distant days was the accompaniment of a noble's feast.

Two days and nights of monastic hospitality being fulfilled,
the Bishop appears to have prolonged his stay at Reading for a
further two days in order to return the Abbot's generous
entertainment.

Venison and three fat does were cooked from the Bishop's store, and partridges also appeared on the menu. There is little doubt whence the game came, as the abbey was but two miles or so from the Manor of Earley which at that time was in the Bishop's hands.

He and his retinue had spent their Christmas at Prestbury. The Festival of the Nativity fell on a Sunday, and after Mass by the Bishop, the day was given over to a sumptuous repast. It was graced with the antique accompaniment of the boar, and prodigious quantities of viands were consumed and lubricated by ten sextaries of red and one of white wine, and an unrecorded quantity of ale.

That the Bishop and his train should, within a few days, be in a condition to do justice to another lavish feast at Reading Abbey, seems altogether remarkable. But so it appears. And

Christmas carolling in the old days, one of the most enduring customs of them all

132

one may only suppose that even in those times, it was the purveyor first and the chirurgeon later.

In the following year, 1958, true to form, Dormer again chose a seasonal theme for his 'Notes and Queries'. On this occasion, his jottings produced a rather unenthusiastic view of the ancient Christmas custom of mumming, and he would no doubt have been surprised if he had known that, almost forty years later, surviving performances in the time-honoured tradition could still be witnessed, not only in Berkshire – as recorded in an earlier chapter – but in many other parts of Britain too.

MUMMING

I do not know whether, during the Christmas season, the Mummers have been at work with their age-old antics. The simple distractions that amused our forefathers would probably be considered boring in an age which has produced television and contemplates a journey to the moon. But within my lifetime I recall quite a number of villages in Berkshire and the adjoining counties where the festive season was enlivened by a presentation of the odd comedy. Swallowfield was a case in point.

Mumming has a very ancient lineage. It is supposed to have been originally instituted in imitation of the *Sigillaria*, or Festival days added to the ancient *Saturnalia*, and was condemned by the Synod of Thurles, where it was decreed that the days called the Calends should be entirely stripped of their ceremonies; that the faithful should no longer observe them; and that the public dancings of women should cease, as being the occasion of much harm and ruin, as being invented and observed in honour of the

gods of the heathens, and therefore quite averse to the Christian life. They therefore decreed that no man should be clothed with a woman's garment, nor any woman with a man's.

While it may be true that the antics performed in the great halls of the English manor houses – there were no community centres in those days – had their origin in the remote Roman festivals, there must have been very many changes and adaptations, both in the presentation and the characters, to produce this rural jantaculum. For the variations in the scores that have come down to us are indicative of local editing and preference.

A few Christmases later, in the early 1960s, Dormer was still not short of a seasonal idea or two when he came to write his column. In this third extract from a remarkable series, he attempts to analyse the traditional Christmas spirit.

The festive season is here again, and with its age-old observances has come the clash of arms in India and the Congo to temper undue exuberance, and this apart from the shadow of a scientific method of man's extermination. Certainly old-time Yuletides did not suffer from the harrowing fears of today.

But it would seem that no strife or danger will ever wholly rob us of those joys with which the Feast of the Nativity has always been associated. Just as distance lends enchantment to the view, so the passing of time brings a heightened richness to the years that are gone.

Already the Edwardian years are taking on something of the glamour of the past, especially to those who recall the quietude of those days. The farther the past recedes, the more glowing its festive accompaniments seem to be. No country

When icy weather coincides with Christmastime, skating is certain
to figure among the 'jovial and carefree distractions' which Ernest
Dormer attributes to the festive season. This was the scene on
Whiteknights Lake, Reading, in the 1940s

inn built today will ever remotely resemble the inns of
Shenstone, Johnson and Dickens; no journey will ever again
have the magic of the Dover Road; and the hens will never
scratch again in the courtyard of the old gabled Lower Ship at
Reading, long since superannuated and taken over by a
modern erection.

What is the strange quality that gives to other days and
other ways a wholly illusory comfort? Why is it that the
wines and ales and cheese and turkeys and mince pies and
plum puddings of yesteryear savour so eloquently of an almost
supernal quality? (Was there ever a mince pie such as that
made by Paice's in Broad Street, Reading, just over a hundred

years ago?) There never was crackling like that roast pig of Charles Lamb; no sack such as that which went the rounds at the Mermaid Tavern, or port at the Cheshire Cheese in Fleet Street; and the feast at Bob Cratchit's can never be conjured again though all the ingredients of that repast be available for the scribe of today.

Like pantomime it all savours of an unreal world. But the reason for this strange attribution of charm and superiority to things that are old, need not unduly bother us; let it suffice that as the season of goodwill comes round, the present joins forces with the past, and from the union come all those jovial and carefree distractions so dear to the heart of every Englishman.

Cold Blows the Winter Wind

TRADITIONAL

Like the other two traditional songs in earlier pages from Alfred Williams's Folk Songs of the Upper Thames, *this example, which at one time was regularly sung in the Berkshire village of Watchfield, was especially popular during the dark winter evenings of the festive season. Singing*

songs of bitter weather in the comfortable warmth of a blazing
yule log no doubt heightened the enjoyment of the occasion,
even if so many of the themes – and this one is no exception –
tugged at the emotions by plumbing the depths of despair. The
first four of the song's many verses give more than a taste of a
poignant tale.

Cold blows the winter's wind, true love,
Cold blow the drops of rain,
The very first love that ever I had,
In greenwood he was slain.

I'll do as much for my true love
As any maiden may,
I'll sit and mourn above his grave
For twelve months and one day.

When twelve months and one day were gone
The spirit began to speak –
'Who's this, who's this upon my grave,
That will not let me sleep?'

''Tis I, 'tis I, your own true love,
A-waiting here for you,
To have one kiss of your lily-white lips,
Which we oft-times used to do.'

The Headstone

C.J.A. BOORMAN

Related in an earlier chapter are some of Berkshire's
strangest stories of the supernatural, based on the personal
accounts of witnesses or on an intriguing mixture of
historical fact and age-old legend. No less spine-chilling are
the tales of mystery created by the county's fiction writers,
for narrating around the Christmas hearth when the nights
are dark and the imagination roams unfettered. The
following story first appeared in the Reading Review *at*
Christmas in 1948.

Trance-like in her high-backed armchair beside the fire, whose light and warmth challenged the poverty of the tiny kitchen and the snow masking the window panes, the old woman sat staring — staring at another high-backed armchair that stood at the opposite end of the hearth, empty.

So she had sat for what seemed an age. Her eyes, set in pools of deep shadow, remained fixed on that other chair as under a spell. Yet all her senses were keyed to the highest pitch of awareness, of expectancy, almost of foreknowledge.

Although it was long past dark, she had not yet lit the lamp nor drawn the blind. Outside the snow was falling: it had fallen all day with the silent, sullen, dogged persistence of destiny. She hated snow. More than the iciness she hated the smothering feel of it. She had been afraid to open the door.

She was also aware that the grandfather clock had stopped — for the first time she could remember. She missed the slow,

measured tick-tock that through the starved years of her married life had been the only friendly tongue she knew. Strange how quiet the place was now.

The old clock, too, was waiting, expectant, sharing her fear. Time was standing still. Time had stood still since . . . *since that other chair had moved.*

It *had* moved. She was sure. Once, twice, ever so little, across the tiled floor. She had heard it; a slight rasping sound. Just the sound it used to make when the old man hitched himself nearer the fire on cold nights. Then she had seen it; a short jerk towards the hearth. Yes, she was sure.

Or was she? The chair was empty. She was sure of that, too. Besides, she had been watching.

No; the old fool she had called husband was dead, buried beneath six feet of solid earth in the grave she had helped him into.

A grave still without a headstone. It ought to have a headstone, for the look of the thing. The village expected it. She had hinted that there would be one, something out of the ordinary – the marble statue of a weeping angel, bowed in frozen grief, like the model in the undertaker's catalogue. She would see to it in the morning.

The chair. It had moved again, the same rasping jerk as before. Yet it was empty still. Her senses were tricking her. How could she be sure of two contradictory things at once?

He was dead all right. How long ago was it? She could not remember. Not long enough anyway. She ought to have done it before. She had wished it often enough.

Years ago, women did do such things by merely wishing. If they were found out they were burned for witchcraft. Nowadays it could not be done by wishing. And wives who killed their husbands were not burned any more: they were hanged. But only if they weren't clever. She had been clever.

When the time came it had been easy. So easy that it looked dead natural. So natural that it deceived everybody, police, coroner and all. So easy and so natural that she wondered why she had not thought of it before.

Miser-like, mortal scared of robbers, he was always fussy about locking the garden gate before going to bed; it was a nightly ritual. First, 'Martha, the lantern!' in that grating, hectoring voice she loathed. Then she would light the candle for him and he would shuffle across the wilderness of garden, leaving the lantern by the well as a beacon and picking it up on the way back.

The well had a good twelve feet of water in it; a long way down. The cover had rotted and fallen in long ago. He would never spend money on a new one. Even in daylight that dark, gaping shaft was dangerous. At night, to one as dim-sighted as he, it was a deathtrap. If the lantern were moved only a little way . . .

So simple to creep out and do it while he was fumbling at the gate. She heard him cry. Wait a minute, to make sure . . . Hurry to the village for help . . . Not too fast . . . Better allow enough time . . .

They had carried him into this very kitchen, all dripping wet. Dead all right. The water had formed a pool in front of the fire, where his chair always stood.

Just as a pool was forming now. There, beneath his chair. Spreading outwards from the hearth. It must be the snow, coming down the chimney . . .

Now he was getting up out of his chair. He was calling for the lantern.

She rose and went to the dresser where the old brass lantern stood. Still with the same piece of candle in it; she had never used it since that night . . .

With shaking fingers she carried the lantern to the fire. She undid the hasp and lit the wick. Then she stood the lantern

on the corner of the rickety table, exactly as she had always done.

'It's ready, Henry.'

So she stood, waiting. What she expected she did not know. She knew only that the wheel of Time had slipped a few cogs, that somehow things were happening as they had happened before.

She looked towards the chair – his chair; at the pool of water beneath, grown larger now, reflecting firelight, red, like blood.

He was at the door; his fingers were on the latch. Then the door, never secure on its worn and rusted hinges, flew open. Snowflakes scurried in on the wind. The fire seemed to shrink to a dull spark as the night framed in the doorway suddenly filled with mist.

Then came silence. Silence so intense that to her crazed mind it passed beyond the borderline of reality and became pregnant with sound. He was calling her; calling; calling.

She took up the lantern, tightened her shawl, and tottered to the door. A wraith of swirling snow enveloped her; then leapt forward, beckoning. She stumbled across the threshold, into the night.

Early next morning the village postman, passing the churchyard, noticed among the tombstones now heaped with snow, one that certainly had not been there the evening before. He stopped and stared. Yes, like a statue. It couldn't be . . . He made his way to the spot, to the grave of the old man accidentally drowned in his own well a year ago. He bent down and brushed away the snow, to gaze in astonishment at the kneeling figure of the widow, bowed in frozen grief, dead as marble, holding an old brass lantern.

Miseries of the
Christmas Holidays

RICHARD DURNFORD

*Although, historically, Eton once lay within the boundaries of
Buckinghamshire, the town was transferred to Berkshire in
the local government reorganisation of 1974 and thus earns a
rightful place in these pages. Eton and its famous school are,
of course, synonymous, and it is from the school's magazine*
The Etonian *of 1821 that the following extract comes. It
was written by a pupil of the day, who, presumably unlike his
modern counterparts, found the Christmas holidays a period of
utter boredom, only relieved by the promise of the start of a
new term.*

As I hate of all things the stiff formality of a crowded drawing
room, I generally enter as late as possible, and creep to a corner,
contenting myself with answering my nearest neighbour.

This, too, is my case at dinner, where most of the
conversation turns upon the transactions of the day; and, since
I have no share in these, of course I cannot enjoy the
description, although it is highly seasoned, and ornamented
with every technical illustration.

Very often a long argument about the conduct of the
County Members, and from thence, by an easy digression, the
late proceedings in Parliament, engross everybody's attention
except mine, for I care as little as may be for either party, and

consider myself totally unfit to form a judgment on any such matters.

The furious spirit and gestures of the combatants please me just in the same way as the contest of prize-fighters do an amateur; besides, the noise overpowers the knives and forks, which are sometimes heard, with an ominous clatter, above the sound of our ordinary conversation.

Some dashing young foxhunter frequently asks me whether we had not a hard run lately at the rebellion? Whether I was in at the death? How many were *spilt*? Upon my answering, as far as I understood him, that I thought it a foolish piece of business, and had nothing to do with it, it is easy to perceive that he sets me down as a *sawney*.

Eton scholars making the most of the wintry weather on Fellows' Pond in 1929

Another inquires, as a piece of general information, how many boys there are at Eton? This is a puzzler, for I never take the trouble to count the list; however, about 500 is nearly sure to be right.

Then I am dreadfully alarmed by a female voice from the top of the table – 'Pray do you know your schoolfellow, Mr Taylor's son?' I immediately excuse myself by observing that there are so many Taylors that it is impossible to distinguish to which of them the lady alludes.

After a minute's interval of consideration, I hear the

An 1880 snowstorm adds a touch of winter beauty to the impressive buildings of Eton College

ominous sound of her friend's Christian name, in a satisfied tone and expression, which is quickly changed for an utterance of surprise when I confess that this only adds to my difficulty; and all the marks of looks, size and disposition are resorted to in vain.

Sometimes I cannot use this evasion, and am obliged to own that I do know a little of the object of inquiry. This is not sufficient; I am expected to understand his temper, his abilities, his character – in fact, to use the querist's expression, 'all about to him'. I find myself placed in a terrible dilemma, between the fear of offending and telling a lie; to get out of which I am, in self defence, obliged to avow that I have but few intimate friends, and that I am not acquainted even by name with half my schoolfellows.

This is certain to astonish everyone, and I am considered, if not a blockhead, at least a very extraordinary and singular youth, and one who has very little intercourse with his equals.

As I neither like wine nor politics, I contrive to steal away, after some time, unperceived from the dessert, and retire to my chamber to compose a few lines of my holiday task, which becomes a pleasure, solely because it is an occupation.

from

The Eternal Stairway

PERCY E. CORBETT

*When Percy Corbett of Newbury published a collection of his
poems in the 1970s under the title* The Eternal Stairway, *he
included this wryly moralistic commentary on contemporary
attitudes towards the festive season, calling it, simply,
'Christmas'.*

Christmas, goodwill and good cheer
Comes, they say, but once a year.
Presents, tinsel, food galore,
All the goods come out of store.
Lots of money needed now,
Parents must find it somehow.
Songs on radio, TV,
All add to the spending spree.
Mincepies, crackers, Christmas cake,
Busy mothers try and bake.
Puddings, holly, mistletoe,
Carols sung where e'er we go.
Turkeys, geese and chicken fine,
Port, gin, sherry and white wine.
Open parcels, eat and drink,

'Carols sung where e'er we go . . . '

Not much time to really think.
Once more mankind intent on bliss,
The hidden beauty tends to miss.
The keynote of it all is love,
Brought to us by the power above,
Beneath, around and in all life,
To overcome problems and strife
E'er present on this planet Earth.
Remember then the divine birth!
Translate the love in kindness true,
In every little act you do.
In every thought and every day,
Help someone on their weary way.
Although we can't all Christlike be,
At least we can each try and *see*.

The Christmas Swimmers

HOWARD BROWNE

For most people, Christmas Day has always been a time to enjoy the comforts of a warm home, relaxing with friends or relatives and making the most of the festive spirit. But in the early years of this century a hardy group of Reading citizens had other ideas. They were all members of the Reading Winter Bathers' Club and, for them, Christmas Day was a very special occasion.

The English have always been thought of as a slightly eccentric race. It's a reputation which can only have been strengthened by the activities indulged in by the members of the Reading Winter Bathers' Club in the early years of the present century.

The club was based at Reading's King's Meadow swimming baths. What made it unusual was that the members shunned the warm days of summer when most rational human beings would normally prefer to go swimming, and instead concentrated their activities to the coldest months of the year. Their season ran from September to the end of April, and during this time an energetic programme of events took place, including monthly racing contests between members.

The intrepid members of the Reading Winter Bathers' Club posed
for this photograph in 1910

These hardy Edwardians were not necessarily all in the
prime of life. One of the more ardent members took an active
part in the club's affairs until he was in his eighties,
swimming along with the rest of them.

Perhaps the most bizarre aspect of the club was the annual
custom of swimming in the Thames on Christmas Day. At the
best of times, even at midsummer, the river is not exactly
tropical in temperature, but in the middle of winter it's
certainly not the most agreeable place to be when all you are
wearing is a pair of bathing trunks.

But the intrepid members of the club were a spartan lot,
and whatever the weather on Christmas Day – snow, frost,
wind or rain – they were not deterred from taking the
obligatory plunge.

Unfortunately, the First World War put a stop to the club's
activities and they were never resumed. The members
dispersed, many no doubt seeing active service, and the
Thames at Christmas was left to flow on its wintry way
undisturbed.

The frozen Thames near Reading Bridge in 1945. Had the Reading
Winter Bathers' Club still been in existence, these were the sort of
conditions which members would have enjoyed for their traditional
Christmas swim, after a little judicious ice-breaking

The Reading Winter Bathers' Club now belongs to the
annals of local history. But at least an early photograph
survives to recall the enthusiastic band of individuals whose
commendable touch of eccentricity bestowed such a
splendid, if unlikely, sparkle to Christmas Day all those
years ago.

Acknowledgements

Introductory sections are by David Green, using published and unpublished reference material and personal interviews.

Beyond the Village Green by Mabel Coppins was published by New Horizon in 1983 and is quoted by courtesy of the author. The extract from *Memories of Old Berkshire* by Jane M. Taylor is reprinted by permission of the Newbury Weekly News Group. The passage from *Village Christmas* (© Miss Read, 1966) is reproduced by permission of the publishers, Michael Joseph Ltd. The items by Queenie Rideout and Edie Fry from *The Book of Wargrave* are included by courtesy of the Wargrave Local History Society. The entries from Queen Victoria's personal journals are reproduced by the gracious permission of Her Majesty the Queen. *Travels Round Our Village* by Eleanor G. Hayden was published by Archibald Constable in 1901. The passage from *Over the Gate* (© Miss Read, 1964) is reproduced by permission of the publishers, Michael Joseph Ltd. The poem 'Christmas Eve, 1916' is from an anthology entitled *Storm in a Village and Other Verses* published by E. Sharwood Smith. The 'Christmas Entertaining' extracts from *The Reading Review* and the story entitled 'The Headstone' by C.J.A. Boorman are reproduced by courtesy of the Berkshire Printing Company. The chapter from *Tales of Old Berkshire* by Cecilia Millson is reprinted by permission of the publishers, Countryside Books. The items from *The Reading Mercury* quoted by William White in 'Christmas Thoughts' are reproduced by courtesy of the Reading Newspaper Company, publishers of *The Reading Chronicle* and formerly publishers of *The Reading Mercury*. The poem 'Christmas' from *The Eternal Stairway* by Percy E. Corbett is reprinted by courtesy of the author's daughter, Mrs Marilyn Leech.

Although considerable effort has been made to trace and contact original authors, this has not proved possible in every case. To those writers who have remained elusive, the compiler and publishers offer grateful acknowledgement for the extracts reproduced.

Picture Credits